The Dawkins
DELUSION?

Atheist Fundamentalism and the Denial of the Divine

Alister E. McGrath *and*
Joanna Collicutt McGrath

IVP Books

An imprint of InterVarsity Press
Downers Grove, Illinois

InterVarsity Press
P.O. Box 1400, Downers Grove, IL 60515-1426
World Wide Web: www.ivpress.com
E-mail: email@ivpress.com

InterVarsity Press® is the book-publishing division of InterVarsity Christian Fellowship/USA®, a student movement active on campus at hundreds of universities, colleges and schools of nursing in the United States of America, and a member movement of the International Fellowship of Evangelical Students. For information about local and regional activities, write Public Relations Dept., InterVarsity Christian Fellowship/USA, 6400 Schroeder Rd., P.O. Box 7895, Madison, WI 53707-7895, or visit the IVCF website at <www.ivcf.org>.

Design: Cindy Kiple

ISBN 978-0-8308-3446-4

Printed in Canada ∞

Library of Congress Cataloging-in-Publication Data

McGrath, Alister E., 1953-
    The Dawkins delusion: atheist fundamentalism and the denial of the
    divine/Alister E. McGrath and Joanna Collicutt McGrath.
        p. cm.
    Includes bibliographical references and index.
    ISBN 978-0-8308-3446-4 (cloth: alk. paper)
    1. Dawkins, Richard, 1941- God delusion. 2. Irreligion. 3.
    Atheism. 4. God. 5. Religion. 6. Apologetics. 7. Faith. I.
    McGrath, Joanna. II. Title.
    BL2775.3.M39 2007
    211'.8—dc22
                           2007116 10

Contents

Introduction.   7

1 Deluded About God?.   17

2 Has Science Disproved God?.   33

3 What Are the Origins of Religion?   53

4 Is Religion Evil?   75

Notes   99

For Further Reading   111

About the Authors   117

Introduction

SINCE THE PUBLICATION OF *THE SELFISH GENE* (1976), Richard Dawkins
has established himself as one of the most successful and skillful
scientific popularizers. Along with his American colleague
Stephen Jay Gould, he has managed to make evolutionary biology
accessible and interesting to a new generation of readers. I and
other admirers of his popular scientific works have long envied
their clarity, their beautiful use of helpful analogies, and their en-
tertaining style.

Yet his latest book marks a significant departure. *The God Delusion* has established Dawkins as the world's most high-profile atheist polemicist, who directs a withering criticism against every form
of religion.[1] He is out to convert his readers: "If this book works as

I intend, religious readers who open it will be atheists when they put it down."[2] Not that he thinks that this is particularly likely; after all, he suggests, "dyed-in-the-wool faith-heads are immune to argument."

Yet the fact that Dawkins has penned a four-hundred-page book declaring that God is a delusion is itself highly significant. *Why is such a book still necessary?* Religion was meant to have disappeared years ago. For more than a century, leading sociologists, anthropologists and psychologists have declared that their children would see the dawn of a new era in which the "God delusion" would be left behind for good. Back in the 1960s, we were told that religion was fading away, to be replaced by a secular world.

For some of us, that sounded like a great thing. I was an atheist back in the late 1960s and remember looking forward to the demise of religion with a certain grim pleasure. I had grown up in Northern Ireland and had known religious tensions and violence at first hand. The solution was obvious to my freethinking mind. Get rid of religion and such tensions and violence would be eradicated. The future was bright—and godless.

Two things have changed since then. In the first place, religion has made a comeback. It is now such a significant element of today's world that it seems strange to think that it was only a generation ago that its death was foretold with such confidence. The humanist writer Michael Shermer, perhaps best known as the director of the Skeptics Society and publisher of *Skeptic* magazine, made this point forcefully back in 1999 when he pointed out that never in history have so many, and such a high percentage of the American population, believed in God.[3] Not only is God not "dead," as the German philosopher Friedrich Nietzsche prematurely proclaimed; he never seems to have been more alive.

Second, and rather less important, my own attitudes have changed. Although I was passionately and totally persuaded of the truth and relevance of atheism as a young man, I subsequently found myself persuaded that Christianity was a much more interesting and intellectually exciting worldview than atheism. I have always valued freethinking and being able to rebel against the orthodoxies of an age. Yet I never suspected where my freethinking would take me.

Dawkins and I have thus traveled in totally different directions, but for substantially the same reasons. We are both Oxford academics who love the natural sciences. Both of us believe passionately in evidence-based thinking and are critical of those who hold passionate beliefs for inadequate reasons. We would both like to think that we would change our minds about God if the evidence demanded it. Yet, on the basis of our experience and analysis of the same world, we have reached radically different conclusions about God. The comparison between us is instructive, yet it raises some difficult questions for Dawkins.

Dawkins, who is presently professor of the public understanding of science at Oxford University, holds that the natural sciences, and especially evolutionary biology, represent an intellectual superhighway to atheism—as they did for him in his youth. In my own case, I started out as an atheist who went on to become a Christian—precisely the reverse of Dawkins's intellectual journey. I had originally intended to spend my life in scientific research but found that my discovery of Christianity led me to study its history and ideas in great depth. I gained my doctorate in molecular biophysics while working in the Oxford laboratories of Professor George Radda, but then gave up active scientific research to study theology.

I have often wondered how Dawkins and I could draw such totally different conclusions on the basis of reflecting long and hard on substantially the same world. One possibility might be that, because I believe in God, I am deranged, deluded, deceived and deceiving, my intellectual capacity having been warped through having been hijacked by an infectious, malignant God virus. Or that, because I am deranged, deluded, deceived and deceiving, my intellectual capacity having been warped through having been hijacked by an infectious, malignant God virus, I believe in God. Both those, I fear, are the substance of the answer I find in the pages of *The God Delusion*.

This may be an answer, but it's not particularly a persuasive answer. It might appeal to diehard atheists whose unbending faith does not permit them to operate outside the "non-God" box. But I hope that I am right in suggesting that such nonthinking dogmatists are not typical of atheism. Another answer to my question might be to repeat the same nonsense, this time applying it to Dawkins. (Although in this case, I suppose that we would have to posit that his mind had been hijacked by some kind of "no-god virus.") But I have no intention of writing something so implausible. Why insult Dawkins? Even more important, why insult the intelligence of my readers?

The beginnings of a real answer lie in some wise words of Stephen Jay Gould, whose sad death from cancer in 2002 robbed

Harvard University of one of its most stimulating teachers, and a popular scientific readership of one of its most accessible writers. Though an atheist, Gould was absolutely clear that the natural sciences—including evolutionary theory—were consistent with both atheism and conventional religious belief. Unless half his scientific colleagues were total fools—a presumption that Gould rightly dismissed as nonsense, whichever half it is applied to—there could be no other responsible way of making sense of the varied responses to reality on the part of the intelligent, informed people that he knew.[4]

This is not the quick and easy answer that many would like. But it may well be right—or at least point in the right direction. It helps us understand why such people hold such fundamentally different beliefs on these matters—and why some others consequently believe that, in the end, these questions cannot be answered with confidence. And it reminds us of the need to treat those who disagree with us on such questions with complete intellectual respect rather than dismissing them as liars, knaves and charlatans.

Whereas Gould at least tries to weigh the evidence, Dawkins simply offers the atheist equivalent of slick hellfire preaching, substituting turbocharged rhetoric and highly selective manipulation of facts for careful, evidence-based thinking. Curiously, there is surprisingly little scientific analysis in *The God Delusion*. There's a lot of pseudoscientific speculation, linked with wider cultural criticisms of religion, mostly borrowed from older atheist writings. Dawkins preaches to his god-hating choirs, who are clearly expected to relish his rhetorical salvoes and raise their hands high in adulation. Those who think biological evolution can be reconciled with religion are dishonest! *Amen!* They belong to the "Neville Chamberlain school" of evolutionists! They are appeasers! *Amen! Real* scientists reject belief in God! *Hallelujah!* The God that Jews believed in back in Old Testament times is a psychotic child abuser! *Amen! You tell them, brother!*

When I read *The God Delusion* I was both saddened and troubled. How, I wondered, could such a gifted popularizer of the natural sciences, who once had such a passionate concern for the objective analysis of evidence, turn into such an aggressive antireligious propagandist with an apparent disregard for evidence that was not favorable to his case? Why were the natural sciences being so abused in an attempt to advance atheist fundamentalism? I have no adequate explanation. Like so many of my atheist friends, I simply cannot understand the astonishing hostility that he displays toward religion. Religion to Dawkins is like a red flag to a bull—evoking not merely an aggressive response but one that throws normal scholarly conventions about scrupulous accuracy and fairness to the winds. While his book is written with rhetorical passion and power, the stridency of its assertions merely masks tired, weak and recycled arguments.

I'm not alone in feeling disappointed here. *The God Delusion* trumpets the fact that its author was recently voted one of the world's three leading intellectuals. This survey took place among the readers of *Prospect* magazine in November 2005. So what did this same magazine make of Dawkins's book? Its reviewer was shocked at this "incurious, dogmatic, rambling, and self-contradictory" book. The title of the review? "Dawkins the Dogmatist."

RESPONDING TO DAWKINS

It is clear that a response of some sort is needed to *The God Delusion,* if only because the absence of one might persuade some that no answer could be given. So how is one to reply? One obvious response would be to write an equally aggressive, inaccurate book, ridiculing atheism by misrepresenting its ideas and presenting its charlatans as if they were its saints. But that would be pointless and counterproductive, not to mention intellectually dishonest.

It is, in fact, actually rather difficult to write a response to this book—but not because it is well-argued or because it marshals such overwhelming evidence in its favor. The book is often little more than an aggregation of convenient factoids suitably overstated to achieve maximum impact and loosely arranged to suggest that they constitute an argument. To rebut this highly selective appeal to evidence would be unspeakably tedious and would simply lead to a hopelessly dull book that seemed tetchy and reactive. Every one of Dawkins's misrepresentations and overstatements can be challenged and corrected. Yet a book that merely offered such a litany of corrections would be catatonically boring. Assuming that Dawkins has equal confidence in all parts of his book, I shall simply challenge him at representative points and let readers draw their own conclusions about the overall reliability of his evidence and judgment.

Dawkins clearly has little interest in engaging religious believers, who will simply find themselves appalled by the flagrant misrepresentation of their beliefs and lifestyles. Is the case for atheism really so weak that it has to be bolstered by such half-baked nonsense? Dawkins pays his readers the highly dubious compliment of assuming that they will share his prejudices and ignorance about religion. Any criticisms of his analysis will simply be met with the riposte: "Well, that's what you *would* say, isn't it?" Objections to his analysis are likely to be dismissed and discounted in advance precisely because they are made by "biased" religious people who are foolish and arrogant enough to criticize "objective" and "rational" atheists.

This is a very serious and troubling point. The total dogmatic conviction of correctness which pervades some sections of Western atheism today—wonderfully illustrated in *The God Delusion*—immediately aligns it with a religious fundamentalism that refuses to allow its ideas to be examined or challenged. Dawkins is resistant to the calibration of his own certainties, seeing them as being luminously true, requiring no defense. He is so convinced that his own views are right that he could not bring himself to believe that the evidence might legitimate any other options—above all, *religious* options.

What is particularly worrying is that, without seeming to realize it, Dawkins simply treats evidence as something to shoehorn into his preconceived theoretical framework. Religion is persistently and consistently portrayed in the worst possible way, mimicking the worst features of religious fundamentalism's portrayal of atheism. When some leading scientists write in support of religion, Dawkins retorts that they simply cannot mean what they say. Dawkins clearly feels deeply threatened by the possibility of his readers encountering religious ideas or people that they might actually like—or even worse, respect and regard as worthy of serious attention.

All this seems to make writing books like this somewhat point-less. *Except that once I too was an atheist and was awaked from my dogmatic slumbers through reading books that challenged my rapidly petrifying worldview.* This book, I suspect, will be read mainly by Christians who want to know what to say to their friends who have read *The God Delusion* and are wondering if believers really are as perverted, degenerate and unthinking as the book makes them out to be. But it is my hope that its readers may include athe-ists whose minds are not yet locked into a pattern of automatic Dawkinsian reflexes. There are many who are deluded about God, and I used to be one of them.

This is a short book, with annotation kept to a minimum to save space. Its primary focus is simple and consistent: a critical engage-ment with the arguments set out in *The God Delusion*. Readers may wish that this book had been expanded to deal with other topics—such as a commendation and exploration of the intellectual resil-ience and spiritual power of Christianity.[5] Those books will be written, in due course. But this one is simple, short and directly to the point. There are no digressions or diversions. It sets out to do one thing and one thing only—assess the reliability of Dawkins's critique of faith in God.[6] Although written in the first person for historical and stylistic reasons, the views and arguments set forth are those of both authors.

But enough by way of introduction. Let us turn immediately to the themes of *The God Delusion*.

1

Deluded About God?

GOD IS A DELUSION—A "PSYCHOTIC DELINQUENT" invented by mad, deluded people.[1] That's the take-home message of *The God Delusion*.
Although Dawkins does not offer a rigorous definition of a *delusion,* he clearly means a belief that is not grounded in evidence—
or, worse, that flies in the face of the evidence. Faith is "blind trust,
in the absence of evidence, even in the teeth of evidence."[2] It is a
"process of non-thinking." It is "evil precisely because it requires
no justification, and brooks no argument."[3] These core definitions
of faith are hardwired into Dawkins's worldview and are obses-
sively repeated throughout his writings. It is not a Christian definition of faith but one that Dawkins has invented to suit his own
polemical purposes. It immediately defines those who believe in

God as people who have lost touch with reality—as those who are *deluded*.

Dawkins rightly notes how important faith is to people. What you believe has a very significant impact on life and thought. That makes it all the more important, we are told, to subject faith to critical, rigorous examination. Delusions need to be exposed—and then removed. I agree entirely. Since the publication of my book *Dawkins' God* in 2004, I am regularly asked to speak on its themes throughout the world. In these lectures, I set out Dawkins's views on religion and then give an evidence-based rebuttal, point by point.

After one such lecture, I was confronted by a very angry young man. The lecture had not been particularly remarkable. I had simply demonstrated, by rigorous use of scientific, historical and philosophical arguments, that Dawkins's intellectual case against God didn't stand up to critical examination. But this man was angry—in fact, I would say he was furious. Why? Because, he told me, wagging his finger agitatedly at me, I had "destroyed his faith." His atheism rested on the authority of Richard Dawkins, and I had totally undermined his faith. He would have to go away and rethink everything. How *dare* I do such a thing!

As I reflected on this event while driving home afterward, I found myself in two minds about this. Part of me regretted the enormous inconvenience that I had clearly caused this person. I had thrown the settled assumptions of his life into turmoil. Yet I consoled myself with the thought that if he was unwise enough to base his life on the clearly inadequate worldview set out by Dawkins, then he would have to realize someday that it rested on decidedly shaky foundations. The dispelling of the delusion had to happen sometime. I just happened to be the historical accident that made it happen at that time and place.

Yet another part of me began to realize how deeply we hold our beliefs, and the impact that they make on everything. Dawkins is right—beliefs are critical. We base our lives on them; they shape our decisions about the most fundamental things. I can still remember the turbulence that I found myself experiencing on making the intellectually painful (yet rewarding) transition from atheism to Christianity. Every part of my mental furniture had to be rearranged. Dawkins is correct—unquestionably correct—when he demands that we should not base our lives on delusions. We all need to examine our beliefs—especially if we are naive enough to think that we don't have any in the first place. But who, I wonder, is really deluded about God?

FAITH IS INFANTILE

As anyone familiar with antireligious polemics knows, a recurring atheist criticism of religious belief is that it is infantile—a childish delusion which ought to have disappeared as humanity reaches its maturity. Throughout his career Dawkins has developed a similar criticism, drawing on a longstanding atheist analogy. In earlier works he emphasized that belief in God is just like believing in the Tooth Fairy or Santa Claus. These are childish beliefs that are abandoned as soon as we are capable of evidence-based thinking. And so is God. It's obvious, isn't it? As Dawkins pointed out in his "Thought for the Day" on BBC Radio in 2003, humanity "can leave the crybaby phase, and finally come of age." This "infantile explanation" belongs to an earlier, superstitious era in the history of humanity. We've outgrown it.[4]

Hmmm. Like many of Dawkins's analogies, this has been constructed with a specific agenda in mind—in this case, the ridiculing of religion. Yet the analogy is obviously flawed. How many people do you know who began to believe in Santa Claus in adulthood? Or who found belief in the Tooth Fairy consoling in old age? I believed in Santa Claus until I was about five (though, not unaware of the benefits it brought, I allowed my parents to think I took it seriously until rather later). I did not believe in God until I started going to university. Those who use this infantile argument have to explain why so many people discover God in later life and certainly do not regard this as representing any kind of regression, perversion or degeneration. A good recent example is provided by Anthony Flew (born 1923), the noted atheist philosopher who started to believe in God in his eighties.

Yet *The God Delusion* is surely right to express concern about the indoctrination of children by their parents.[5] Innocent minds are corrupted by adults cramming their religious beliefs down their children's throats. Dawkins argues that the biological process of natural selection builds child brains with a tendency to believe whatever their parents or elders tell them. This, he suggests, makes them prone to trust whatever a parent says—like Santa Claus. This is seen as one of the most significant factors involved in sustaining religious belief in the world, when it ought to have been wiped out ages ago. Break the intergenerational cycle of the transmission of religious ideas, and that will put an end to this nonsense. Bringing up children within a religious tradition, he suggests, is a form of child abuse.

There is, of course, a reasonable point being made here. Yet somehow, it gets lost in the noise of the hyped-up rhetoric and a general failure to consider its implications. Having read the misrepresentations of religion that are such a depressing feature of *The God Delusion,* I very much fear that secularists would merely force their own dogmas down the throats of the same gullible children—who lack, as Dawkins rightly points out, the discriminatory capacities needed to evaluate the ideas. I do not wish to be unkind, but this whole approach sounds uncomfortably like the antireligious programs built into the education of Soviet children during the 1950s, based on mantras such as "Science has disproved religion!" "Religion is superstition!" and the like.

There is indeed a need for a society to reflect on how it educates its children. Yet no case can be made for them to be force-fed Dawkins's favored dogmas and distortions. They need to be told, fairly and accurately, what Christianity actually teaches—rather than be subjected to the derisory misrepresentations of Christian theology that litter this piece of propaganda. *The God Delusion,* more by its failings than its achievements, reinforces the need for high-quality religious education in the public arena, countering the crude caricatures, prejudicial stereotypes and blatant misrepresentations now being aggressively peddled by atheist fundamentalism.

For many years I gave a series of lectures at Oxford University titled "An Introduction to Christian Theology." I cannot help but feel that these might have been of some use to Dawkins in writing his book. As the cultural and literary critic Terry Eagleton pointed out in his withering review of *The God Delusion:* "Imagine someone holding forth on biology whose only knowledge of the subject is the *Book of British Birds,* and you have a rough idea of what it feels like to read Richard Dawkins on theology."[6]

Dawkins quotes with approval the views of his friend Nicholas Humphrey, who suggests that parents should no more be allowed to teach children about the "literal truth of the Bible" than "to knock their children's teeth out."[7] If Humphrey is consistent here, he should be equally outraged about those who peddle misrepresentations of religion as if they were the truth. Might he argue, I wonder, that parents who read *The God Delusion* aloud to their children were also committing child abuse? Or are you only abusive if you impose religious, but not antireligious, dogmas and delusions?

FAITH IS IRRATIONAL

There is, I suppose, a lunatic fringe to every movement. Having been involved in many public debates over whether science has disproved the existence of God, I have ample experience of what I think I must describe as somewhat weird people, often with decidedly exotic ideas, on both sides of the God-atheism debate. One of the most characteristic features of Dawkins's antireligious polemic is to present the pathological as if it were normal, the fringe as if it were the center, crackpots as if they were mainstream. It generally works well for his intended audience, who can be assumed to know little about religion and probably care for it even less. But it's not acceptable. And it's certainly not scientific.

Dawkins insists that Christian belief is "a persistently false belief held in the face of strong contradictory evidence."[8] The problem is how to persuade "dyed-in-the wool faith-heads" that atheism is right, when they are so deluded by religion that they are immune to any form of rational argument. Faith is thus essentially and irredeemably irrational. In support of his case Dawkins has sought out Christian theologians who he believes will substantiate this fundamentally degenerate aspect of religious faith. In earlier writings he asserted that the third-century Christian writer Tertullian said some particularly stupid things, including "it is by all means to be believed because it is absurd." This is dismissed as typical religious nonsense. "That way madness lies."[9]

He's stopped quoting this now, I am pleased to say, after I pointed out that Tertullian actually said no such thing. Dawkins had fallen into the trap of not checking his sources and merely repeating what older atheist writers had said. It's yet another wearisome example of the endless recycling of outdated arguments that has become so characteristic of atheism in recent years.

However, Dawkins now seems to have found a new example of the irrationalism of faith—well, new for him, at any rate. In *The God Delusion* he cites a few choice snippets from the sixteenth-century German Protestant writer Martin Luther, culled from the Internet, demonstrating Luther's anxieties about reason in the life of faith.[10] No attempt is made to clarify what Luther means by *reason* and how it differs from what Dawkins takes to be the self-evident meaning of the word.[11]

What Luther was actually pointing out was that human reason could never fully take in a central theme of the Christian faith—that God should give humanity the wonderful gift of salvation without demanding they do something for him first. Left to itself, human common sense would conclude that you need to do something to earn God's favor—an idea that Luther regarded as compromising the gospel of divine graciousness, making salvation something that you earned or merited.

Dawkins's inept engagement with Luther shows how Dawkins abandons even the pretense of rigorous evidence-based scholarship. Anecdote is substituted for evidence; selective Internet trawling for quotes displaces rigorous and comprehensive engagement with primary sources. In this book, Dawkins throws the conventions of academic scholarship to the winds; he wants to write a work of propaganda and consequently treats the accurate rendition of religion as an inconvenient impediment to his chief agenda, which is the intellectual and cultural destruction of religion. It's an unpleasant characteristic that he shares with other fundamentalists.

ARGUMENTS FOR GOD'S EXISTENCE?

Dawkins holds that the existence or nonexistence of God is a scientific hypothesis which is open to rational demonstration. In *The Blind Watchmaker,* he provided a sustained and effective critique of the arguments of the nineteenth-century writer William Paley for the existence of God on biological grounds. It is Dawkins's home territory, and he knows what he is talking about. This book remains the finest criticism of this argument in print.[12] The only criticism I would direct against this aspect of *The Blind Watchmaker* is that Paley's ideas were typical of his age, not of Christianity as a whole, and that many Christian writers of the age were alarmed at his approach, seeing it as a surefire recipe for the triumph of atheism. There is no doubt in my mind that Paley saw himself as in some way "proving" the existence of God, and Dawkins's extended critique of Paley in that book is fair, gracious and accurate.

In *The God Delusion,* Dawkins turns his attention to such other "arguments" based on the philosophy of religion. I am not sure that this was entirely wise. He is clearly out of his depth, and achieves little by his brief and superficial engagement with these great perennial debates, which often simply cannot be resolved empirically.[13] His attitude seems to be "here's how a scientist would sort out this philosophical nonsense."

For example, Dawkins takes issue with the approaches developed by Thomas Aquinas in the thirteenth century, traditionally known as the "Five Ways."[14] The general consensus is that while such arguments cast interesting light on the questions, they settle nothing. Although traditionally referred to as "arguments for God's existence," this is not an accurate description. All they do is show the inner consistency of belief in God—in much the same way as the classic arguments for atheism (such as Ludwig Feuerbach's famous idea of the "projection" of God; see p. 54) demonstrate its inner consistency, but not its evidential foundations.

The basic line of thought guiding Thomas is that the world mirrors God, as its Creator. It is an assumption derived from faith, which Thomas argues to resonate with what we observe in the world. For example, its signs of ordering can be explained on the basis of the existence of God as its creator. This approach is still widely encountered in Christian writings which argue that an existing faith in God offers a better "empirical fit" with the world than its alternatives. As Dawkins himself uses this same approach to commend atheism elsewhere, I cannot really see that he has much to complain about here.

At no point does Thomas speak of these as being "proofs" for God's existence; rather they are to be seen as a demonstration of the inner coherence of belief in God. Thomas is interested in exploring the rational implications of faith in terms of our experience of beauty, causality and so forth. Belief in God is actually assumed; it is then shown that this belief makes sense of what may be observed within the world. The appearance of design can offer persuasion, not proof, concerning the role of divine creativity in the universe. Dawkins misunderstands an a posteriori demonstration of the coherence of faith and observation to be an a priori proof of faith—an entirely understandable mistake for those new to this field, but a serious error nonetheless.

Where Dawkins sees faith as intellectual nonsense, most of us are aware that we hold many beliefs that we cannot prove to be true but are nonetheless perfectly reasonable to entertain.[15] To lapse into jargon for a moment: our beliefs may be shown to be *justifiable,* without thereby demonstrating that they are *proven.* This is not a particularly difficult or obscure point. Philosophers of science have long made the point that there are many scientific theories that are presently believed to be true but may have to be discarded in the future as additional evidence emerges or new theoretical interpretations develop. There is no difficulty, for example, in believing that Darwin's theory of evolution is presently the best explanation of the available evidence, but that doesn't mean it is correct.[16]

THE EXTREME IMPROBABILITY OF GOD

Dawkins devotes an entire chapter to an argument—or, more accurately, a loosely collated series of assertions—to the general effect that "there almost certainly is no God."[17] This rambling pastiche is poorly structured, making it quite difficult to follow its basic argument, which seems to be an expansion of the "who made God, then?" question. "Any God capable of designing anything would have to be complex enough to demand the same kind of explanation in his own right. God presents an infinite regress from which he cannot help us to escape."[18]

Dawkins is particularly derisive about theologians who allow themselves "the dubious luxury of arbitrarily conjuring up a terminator to an infinite regress."[19] Anything that explains something itself has to be explained—and *that* explanation in turn needs to be explained, and so on. There is no justifiable way of ending this infinite regression of explanations. What explains the explanation? Or, to change the metaphor slightly: Who designed the designer?

However, it needs to be pointed out here that the holy grail of the natural sciences is the quest for the "grand unified theory"—the "theory of everything." Why is such a theory regarded as being so important? Because it can explain everything, without itself requiring or demanding an explanation.[20] The explanatory buck stops right there. There is no infinite regress in the quest for explanation. If Dawkins's brash and simplistic arguments carried weight, this great scientific quest could be dismissed with a seemingly profound yet in fact trivial question: What explains the explainer?

Now maybe there is no such ultimate theory. Maybe the "theory of everything" will turn out to be a "theory of nothing." Yet there is no reason to suppose that this quest is a failure from the outset simply because it represents the termination of an explanatory process. Yet an analogous quest for an irreducible explanation lies at the heart of the scientific quest. There is no logical inconsistency, no conceptual flaw, no self-contradiction involved.

Dawkins then sets out an argument that makes little sense, either in the brief and hasty statement offered in *The God Delusion* or the more expanded versions he set out elsewhere. In a somewhat patchy and derisory account of the "anthropic principle," Dawkins points out the sheer improbability of our existence. Belief in God, he then argues, represents belief in a being whose existence must be even more complex—and therefore more improbable. Yet this leap from the recognition of complexity to the assertion of improbability is highly problematic. Why is something complex improbable? A "theory of everything" may well be more complex than the lesser theories that it explains—but what has that to do with its improbability?

But let's pause for a moment. The one inescapable and highly improbable fact about the world is that we, as reflective human beings, are in fact here. Now it is virtually impossible to quantify how improbable the existence of humanity is. Dawkins himself is clear, especially in *Climbing Mount Improbable,* that it is very, very improbable.[21] *But we are here.* The very fact that we are puzzling about how we came to be here is dependent on the fact that we are here and are thus able to reflect on the likelihood of this actuality. Perhaps we need to appreciate that there are many things that seem improbable—but improbability does not, and never has, entailed nonexistence. *We* may be highly improbable—*yet we are here*. The issue, then, is not whether God is *probable* but whether God is *actual*.

THE GOD OF THE GAPS

In *The God Delusion* Dawkins criticizes "the worship of gaps." This is a reference to an approach to Christian apologetics that came to prominence during the eighteenth and nineteenth centuries—the so-called God of the gaps approach.[22] In its simplest form it asserted that there were necessarily "gaps" in a naturalist or scientific understanding of reality. At certain points, William Paley's famous *Natural Theology* (1801) uses arguments along these lines. It was argued that God needs to be proposed in order to deal with these gaps in scientific understanding.

It was a foolish move and was increasingly abandoned in the twentieth century. Oxford's first professor of theoretical chemistry, the noted Methodist lay preacher Charles A. Coulson, damned it with the telling phrase "the God of the gaps." In its place he urged a comprehensive account of reality, which stressed the explanatory capacity of the Christian faith as a whole rather than a retreat into ever-diminishing gaps.[23] Dawkins's criticism of those who "worship the gaps," despite its overstatements, is clearly appropriate and valid. So we must thank him for helping us kill off this outdated false turn in the history of Christian apologetics. It is a good example of how a dialogue between science and Christian theology can lead to some useful outcomes.

Unfortunately, having made such a good point, Dawkins then weakens his argument by suggesting that all religious people try to stop scientists from exploring those gaps: "one of the truly bad effects of religion is that it teaches us that it is a virtue to be satisfied with not understanding."[24] While that may be true of some more exotic forms of Christian theology, it is most emphatically not characteristic of its approaches. It's a crass generalization that ruins a perfectly interesting discussion.

After all, there is nothing wrong with admitting limits to our understanding, partly arising from the limits of science itself, and partly from the limited human capacity to comprehend. As Dawkins himself pointed out elsewhere: "Modern physics teaches us that there is more to truth than meets the eye; or than meets the all too limited human mind, evolved as it was to cope with medium-sized objects moving at medium speeds through medium distances in Africa."[25]

It's hardly surprising that this "all too limited" human mind should encounter severe difficulties when dealing with anything beyond the world of everyday experience. The idea of "mystery" arises constantly as the human mind struggles to grasp some ideas. That's certainly true of science; it's also true of religion.

The real problem here, however, is the forced relocation of God by doubtless well-intentioned Christian apologists into the hidden recesses of the universe, beyond evaluation or investigation. Now that's a real concern. For this strategy is still used by the intelligent design movement—a movement, based primarily in North America, that argues for an "intelligent Designer" based on gaps in scientific explanation, such as the "irreducible complexity" of the world. It is not an approach which I accept, either on scientific or theological grounds. In my view, those who adopt this approach make Christianity deeply—and needlessly—vulnerable to scientific progress.

But the "God of the gaps" approach is only one of many Christian approaches to the question of how the God hypothesis makes sense of things. In my view it was misguided; it was a failed apologetic strategy from an earlier period in history that has now been rendered obsolete. This point has been taken on board by Christian theologians and philosophers of religion throughout the twentieth century who have now reverted to older, more appropriate ways of dealing with this question. For instance, the Oxford philosopher Richard Swinburne is one of many writers to argue that the capacity of science to explain itself requires explanation— and that the most economical and reliable account of this explanatory capacity lies in the notion of a Creator God.[26]

Swinburne's argument asserts that the intelligibility of the universe itself needs explanation. It is therefore not the *gaps* in our understanding of the world which point to God but rather the very *comprehensibility* of scientific and other forms of understanding that requires an explanation. In brief, the argument is that *explicability itself requires explanation*. The more scientific advance is achieved, the greater will be our understanding of the universe— and hence the greater need to explain this very success. It is an approach which commends and encourages scientific investigation, not seeks to inhibit it.

But what of the relationship of science and religion more generally? Dawkins has had much to say on this, and we must move on to consider it.

2

Has Science Disproved God?

UNDERLYING THE AGENDA OF *THE GOD DELUSION* is a pervasive belief that science has disproved God. Those who continue to believe in God are simply obscurantist, superstitious reactionaries, who are in complete denial about the victorious advance of the sciences, which have eliminated God from even the most minuscule gaps in our understanding of the universe. Atheism is the only option for the serious, progressive, thinking person.

But it's not that simple—and just about every natural scientist that I have talked to about this issue knows this. We have already noted Stephen Jay Gould's rejection of any brash equation of scientific excellence with an atheist faith. As Gould observed in *Rocks of Ages,* based on the religious views of leading evolutionary biologists: "Either half my colleagues are enormously stupid, or else the science of Darwinism is fully compatible with conventional religious beliefs—and equally compatible with atheism."[1] As I pointed out in *Dawkins' God,* his point is fair and widely accepted: nature can be interpreted in a theistic or in an atheistic way—but it demands neither of these. Both are genuine intellectual possibilities for science.

The fact that America's leading evolutionary biologist should make such a statement outrages Dawkins. How could he say such a thing! Dawkins dismisses Gould's thoughts without giving them serious consideration. "I simply do not believe that Gould could possibly have meant much of what he wrote in *Rocks of Ages.*"[2] This creedal statement is Dawkins's substitute for a response. It simply will not do. For Gould has simply articulated the widely held view that there are limits to science. The same view, much to Dawkins's irritation, is found in Martin Rees's admirable *Cosmic Habitat,* which (entirely reasonably) points out that some ultimate questions "lie beyond science."[3] As Rees is the president of the Royal Society, which brings together Britain's leading scientists, his comments deserve careful and critical attention.

The fundamental issue confronting the sciences is how to make sense of a highly complex, multifaceted, multilayered reality. This fundamental question in human knowledge has been much discussed by philosophers of science, and often ignored by those who, for their own reasons, want to portray science as the only viable route to genuine knowledge. Above all, it pulls the rug out from under those who want to talk simplistically about scientific "proof" or "disproof" of such things as the meaning of life or the existence of God. The natural sciences depend on inductive infer-ence, which is a matter of "weighing evidence and judging proba-bility, not of proof."[4] Competing explanations are evident at every level of the human endeavor to represent the world—from the de-tails of quantum mechanics to what Karl Popper termed "ultimate questions" of meaning.

This means that the great questions of life (some of which are also scientific questions) cannot be answered with any degree of cer-tainty. Any given set of observations can be explained by a number of theories. To use the jargon of the philosophy of science: theories are underdetermined by the evidence. The question then arises: what criteria can be used to decide between them, especially when they are "empirically equivalent"? Simplicity? Beauty? The debate rages, unresolved. And its outcome is entirely to be expected: the great questions remain unanswered. There can be no question of scientific "proof" of ultimate questions. Either we cannot answer them or we must answer them on grounds other than the sciences.

THE LIMITS OF SCIENCE?

Science is the only reliable tool that we possess to understand the world. It has no limits. We may not know something now—but we will in the future. It is just a matter of time. This view, found throughout Dawkins's body of writings, is given added emphasis in *The God Delusion*, which offers a vigorous defense of the univer-sal scope and conceptual elegance of the natural sciences. It is an idea that is by no means specific to Dawkins, who here both re-flects and extends a reductive approach to reality found in earlier writers such as Francis Crick.[5] The point is simple: there are no "gaps" in which God can hide. Science will explain everything—including why some still believe in such a ridiculous idea as God. Yet it is an approach that simply cannot be sustained, either as representative of the scientific community or as a self-evidently correct position, irrespective of what that community makes of it.

To avoid misunderstanding, let's be quite clear that suggesting that science may have its limits is in no way a criticism or defamation of the scientific method. Dawkins does, I have to say with regret, tend to portray anyone raising questions about the scope of the sciences as a science-hating idiot. Yet there is a genuine question here. Every intellectual tool that we possess needs to be calibrated—in other words, to be examined to identify the conditions under which it is reliable. The question of whether science has limits is certainly not improper, nor does a positive answer to the question in any way represent a lapse into some kind of superstition. It is simply a legitimate demand for calibration of intellectual accuracy.

To explore this question, let's consider a statement made by Dawkins in his first work, *The Selfish Gene*.

> [Genes] swarm in huge colonies, safe inside gigantic lumbering robots, sealed off from the outside world, communicating with it by tortuous indirect routes, manipulating it by remote control. They are in you and me; they created us, body and mind; and their preservation is the ultimate rationale for our existence.[6]

We see here a powerful and influential interpretation of a basic scientific concept. But are these strongly interpretative statements themselves actually *scientific*?

To appreciate the issue, consider the following rewriting of this paragraph by the celebrated Oxford physiologist and systems biologist Denis Noble. What is proven empirical fact is retained; what is interpretative has been changed, this time offering a somewhat different reading of things.

> [Genes] are trapped in huge colonies, locked inside highly intelligent beings, moulded by the outside world, communicating with it by complex processes, through which, blindly, as if by magic, function emerges. They are in you and me; we are the system that allows their code to be read; and their preservation is totally dependent on the joy that we experience in reproducing ourselves. We are the ultimate rationale for their existence.[7]

Dawkins and Noble see things in completely different ways. (I recommend reading both statements slowly and carefully to appreciate the difference.) They simply cannot both be right. Both smuggle in a series of quite different value judgments and metaphysical statements. Yet their statements are "empirically equivalent." In other words, they both have equally good grounding in observation and experimental evidence. So which is right? Which is more scientific? How could we decide which is to be preferred on scientific grounds? As Noble observes—and Dawkins concurs—"no-one seems to be able to think of an experiment that would detect an empirical difference between them."[8]

In a sophisticated recent critique of the philosophical shallowness of much contemporary scientific writing, particularly in the neurosciences, Max Bennett and Peter Hacker direct particular

criticism against the naive "science explains everything" outlook
that Dawkins seems determined to advance.[9] Scientific theories
cannot be said to "explain the world"—they only explain the *phenomena* that are observed within the world. Furthermore, they argue, scientific theories do not and are not intended to describe and
explain "everything about the world"—such as its purpose. Law,
economics and sociology can be cited as examples of disciplines
which engage with domain-specific phenomena without in any
way having to regard themselves as somehow being inferior to or
dependent on the natural sciences.

Yet most important, there are many questions that by their very
nature must be recognized to lie beyond the legitimate scope of the
scientific method, as this is normally understood. For example, is
there purpose within nature? Dawkins regards this as a spurious
nonquestion. Yet this is hardly an illegitimate question for human
beings to ask or to hope to have answered. Bennett and Hacker
point out that the natural sciences are not in a position to comment
on this if their methods are applied legitimately.[10] The question
cannot be dismissed as illegitimate or nonsensical; it is simply being declared to lie beyond the scope of the scientific method. If it
can be answered, it must be answered on other grounds.

This point was made repeatedly by Peter Medawar, an Oxford
immunologist who won the Nobel Prize for medicine for the discovery of acquired immunological tolerance. In a significant publication titled *The Limits of Science,* Medawar explored the question
of how science was limited by the nature of reality. Emphasizing
that "science is incomparably the most successful enterprise human beings have ever engaged upon," he distinguishes between

what he calls "transcendent" questions, which are better left to religion and metaphysics, and questions about the organization and structure of the material universe. With regard to the latter, he argues, there are no limits to the possibilities of scientific achievement. He thus agrees with Dawkins—but only by defining and limiting the domain within which the sciences possess such competency.

So what of other questions? What about the question of God? Or of whether there is purpose within the universe? As if preempting Dawkins's brash and simplistic take on the sciences, Medawar suggests that scientists need to be cautious about their pronouncements on these matters lest they lose the trust of the public by confident and dogmatic overstatements. Though a self-confessed rationalist, Medawar is clear on this matter:

> That there is indeed a limit upon science is made very likely by the existence of questions that science cannot answer, and that no conceivable advance of science would empower it to answer. . . . I have in mind such questions as:
>
> How did everything begin?
> What are we all here for?
> What is the point of living?
> Doctrinaire positivism—now something of a period piece—dismissed all such questions as nonquestions or pseudoquestions such as only simpletons ask and only charlatans profess to be able to answer.[11]

Perhaps *The God Delusion* might have taken Medawar by surprise, on account of its late flowering of precisely that "doctrinaire positivism" which he had, happily yet apparently prematurely, believed to be dead.

NOMAs AND POMAs

Our brief discussion of the limits of science suggests that the natural sciences, philosophy, religion and literature all have a legitimate place in the human quest for truth and meaning. This is a widely held view, both in Western culture at large and even within many sections of the scientific community itself. However, it is not universally held within that community. The somewhat ugly term *scientism* has now emerged to designate those natural scientists who refuse to concede any limits to the sciences—such as Dawkins.[12] The issues are encountered at several points in *The God Delusion*, especially in Dawkins's critique of Stephen Jay Gould's idea of the NOMA (nonoverlapping magisteria) of science and religion.

On Gould's view the "magisterium of science" deals with the "empirical realm," whereas the "magisterium of religion" deals with "questions of ultimate meaning." (The term *magisterium* is best understood as a "sphere of authority" or "domain of competency.") Gould holds that these two magisteria do not overlap. I think he's wrong. Dawkins also thinks he's wrong, although for rather different reasons. For Dawkins there is only one *magisterium*—empirical reality. This is the only reality that exists. The idea of allowing theology to speak about anything is outrageous. "Why are scientists so cravenly respectful towards the ambitions of theologians, over questions that theologians are certainly no more qualified to answer than scientists themselves?"[13] It's an interesting piece of rhetoric, but it doesn't even begin to address the issues that Gould rightly raised but answered wrongly.

For there is, of course, a third option—that of "partially over-lapping magisteria" (a POMA, so to speak), reflecting a realization that science and religion offer possibilities of cross-fertilization on account of the interpenetration of their subjects and methods. One obvious exponent of this view is Francis Collins, an evolutionary biologist who heads up the famous Human Genome Project. Collins speaks of "a richly satisfying harmony between the scientific and spiritual worldviews."[14] "The principles of faith are," he suggests, "complementary with the principles of science." Others can easily be cited, from many scientific disciplines, making substantially the same point. In my own "scientific theology" project I explore how theology can learn from the methodology of the natural sciences in exploring and developing its ideas.[15] This approach of "overlapping magisteria" is implicit in the philosophy of "critical realism," which is currently having such an impact on illuminating the relationship of the natural and social sciences.[16]

It's not Gould versus Dawkins here, as if these two positions define the only intellectual options available to us. At times, Dawkins seems to assume that discrediting Gould necessarily implies the validation of his own position. The reality, however, is that Gould and Dawkins represent only two positions on a broad spectrum of possibilities already well known to scholarship. The inadequacies of both suggest that these alternatives merit closer examination in the future.

THE WARFARE OF SCIENCE AND RELIGION?

Science has, in Dawkins's view, wrecked faith in God, relegating God to the margins of culture, where he is embraced by deluded fanatics. There's an obvious problem, of course—namely, that rather a lot of scientists do believe in God. *The God Delusion* was published in 2006. In that same year three other books were published by leading research scientists. Owen Gingerich, a noted Harvard astronomer, produced *God's Universe,* declaring that "the universe has been created with intention and purpose, and that this belief does not interfere with the scientific enterprise."[17] Francis Collins published his *Language of God,* which argues that the wonder and ordering of nature points to a Creator God, very much along the lines of the traditional Christian conception. In this book Collins describes his own conversion from atheism to Christian faith. This hardly fits Dawkins's rigid insistence that real scientists are atheists.

A few months later the cosmologist Paul Davies published his *Goldilocks Enigma,* arguing for the existence of "fine-tuning" in the universe. For Davies, the bio-friendliness of the universe points to an overarching principle that somehow pushes the universe toward the development of life and mind. The idea that there is any evidence of purpose or design in the universe is, of course, dismissed out of hand by Dawkins. Davies has other ideas. While not subscribing to a traditional Christian notion of God, there's something divine out there. Or maybe in there.

Some surveys help cast at least a little light on this. Back in 1916, active scientists were asked whether they believed in God—specifically, a God who actively communicates with humanity and to whom one may pray "in expectation of receiving an answer." Deists don't believe in God, by this definition. The results are well-known: roughly 40 percent did believe in this kind of God, 40 percent did not and 20 percent were not sure. The survey was re-

peated in 1997, using precisely the same question, and found
pretty much the same pattern, with a slight increase in those who
did not (up to 45 percent). The number of those who did believe
in such a God remained stable at about 40 percent.

These results, of course, can be spun in all kinds of ways. Atheists tend to interpret them to say "most scientists don't believe in
God." It's not that simple. It could equally be interpreted to mean
"most scientists do not disbelieve in God," in that 55 percent either believe in God or are agnostic. Two points, however, must be
borne in mind.

1. James Leuba, who conducted the original survey in 1916, pre-
   dicted that the number of scientists disbelieving in God would
   rise significantly over time, as a result of general improvements
   in education. There is a small increase in the number of those
   who disbelieve and a corresponding diminution in those who are
   agnostic—but not any significant reduction in those who believe.
2. Once more, it must be emphasized that scientists were asked a
   highly specific question, namely, did those questioned believe
   in a personal God who might be expected to answer prayer?
   This rules out all those who believe that the evidence points to
   some kind of deity or supreme spiritual principle—such as Paul
   Davies. If the question had been framed in more general terms,
   a larger positive response might be expected on both occasions.
   The precise nature of this question is often overlooked by those
   commenting on both the 1916 and 1997 results.

But the fine details of such surveys are actually beside the point.
Dawkins is forced to contend with the highly awkward fact that
his view that the natural sciences are an intellectual superhighway

to atheism is rejected by most scientists, irrespective of their religious views. Most unbelieving scientists of my acquaintance are
atheists on grounds other than their science; they bring those assumptions *to* their science rather than basing them *on* their science. Indeed, if my own personal conversations are anything to go
by, some of Dawkins's most vociferous critics among scientists are
actually atheists. His dogmatic insistence that all "real" scientists
ought to be atheists has met with fierce resistance from precisely
the community that he believes should be his fiercest and most
loyal supporter. Dawkins clearly has no mandate whatsoever to
speak for the scientific community at this point or on this topic.
There is a massive observational discrepancy between the number
of scientists that Dawkins believes should be atheists and those
who are so in practice.

Dawkins deals with this problem in a thoroughly unacceptable
manner. For instance, consider his remarks about Freeman Dyson,
a physicist widely tipped to win a Nobel Prize for his ground-
breaking work in quantum electrodynamics. On being awarded
the Templeton Prize in Religion in 2000, Dyson gave an acceptance speech celebrating the achievements of religion, while noting (and criticizing) its downside. He was also clear about the
downside of atheism, noting that "the two individuals who epito-
mized the evils of our century, Adolf Hitler and Joseph Stalin, were
both avowed atheists." Dawkins regarded this as a craven act of
apostasy and betrayal, offering "an endorsement of religion by one
of the world's most distinguished physicists."[18]

But worse was to come. When Dyson commented that he was a
Christian who wasn't particularly interested in the doctrine of the

Trinity, Dawkins insisted that this meant that Dyson wasn't a Christian at all. He was just *pretending* to be religious! "Isn't that just what any atheistic scientist *would* say, if he wanted to sound Christian?"[19] Is the implication that Dyson is being meretriciously compliant, feigning an interest in religion for financial gain? Is Dawkins saying that Dyson just wanted to "sound" Christian, when he was really an atheist? The same is true of Einstein, who often used religious language and imagery in his accounts of science.[20]

Here, as elsewhere, Dawkins is driven by his core assumption that *real scientists must be atheists*. They simply cannot mean it when they own up to religious beliefs, interests or commitments. I'm not sure what kind of people Dawkins hopes to persuade with this refusal to believe his fellow scientists. It just represents the triumph of dogma over observation.

So why are so many scientists religious? The obvious and most intellectually satisfying explanation of this is not difficult to identify. It is well known that the natural world is conceptually malleable. It can be interpreted, without any loss of intellectual integrity, in a number of different ways. Some read or interpret nature in an atheist way. Others read it in a deistic way, seeing it as pointing to a Creator divinity, who is no longer involved in its affairs. God winds up the clock, then leaves it to work on its own. Others take a more specifically Christian view, believing in a God who both creates and sustains. Others take a more spiritualized view, speaking more vaguely of some "life force."

The point is simple: nature is open to many legitimate interpretations. It can be interpreted in atheist, deist, theist and many other ways—but it does not demand to be interpreted in any of these. One can be a "real" scientist without being committed to any specific religious, spiritual or antireligious view of the world. This, I may add, is the view of most scientists I speak to, including those who self-define as atheists. Unlike dogmatic atheists, they can understand perfectly well why some of their colleagues adopt a Christian view of the world. They may not agree with that approach, but they're prepared to respect it.

Dawkins, however, has a radically different view. Science and religion are locked into a battle to the death.[21] Only one can emerge victorious—and it must be science. The Dawkinsian view of reality is a mirror image of that found in some of the more exotic sections of American fundamentalism. The late Henry Morris, a noted creationist, saw the world as absolutely polarized into two factions. The saints were the religious faithful (which Morris defined in his own rather exclusive way). The evil empire consisted of atheist scientists. Morris offered an apocalyptic vision of this battle, seeing it as being cosmic in its significance. It was all about truth versus falsehood, good versus evil. And in the end, truth and good would triumph! Dawkins simply replicates this fundamentalist scenario, while inverting its frame of reference.

It is a hopelessly muddled reading of things. It ultimately depends on an obsolete and now abandoned historical reading of the relationship of science and religion. Once upon a time, back in the second half of the nineteenth century, it was certainly possible to believe that science and religion were permanently at war. Yet, as one of America's leading historians of science recently remarked to me, this is now seen as a hopelessly outmoded historical stereotype that scholarship has totally discredited. It lingers on only in the backwaters of intellectual life, where the light of scholarship has yet to penetrate. The relationship between science and religion is complex and variegated—but it could never conceivably be represented as a state of total war.

Yet Dawkins is so unswervingly committed to this obsolete warfare model that he is led to make some very unwise and indefensible judgments. The most ridiculous of these is that scientists who believe in or contribute to a positive working relationship between science and religion represent the "Neville Chamberlain" school.[22] This comparison is intellectual nonsense, not to mention personally offensive. For those readers who do not recognize the allusion, Dawkins is here referring to the policy of appeasement that the British prime minister Neville Chamberlain adopted toward Adolf Hitler in 1938, in the hope of avoiding total war in Europe. The distasteful analogy seems to imply that scientists who affirm the importance of religion are to be stigmatized as "appeasers," and that religious people are to be compared, equally offensively, to Hitler. Dawkins's imagery here seems to express some alarmingly prejudiced and poorly informed judgments about the relationship of science and religion.

So who does Dawkins have in mind? Incredibly, he singles out Michael Ruse—a distinguished atheist philosopher who has done much to clarify the philosophical roots and consequences of Darwinism, and to challenge religious fundamentalism.[23] Why? Dawkins's argument is so muddled here that it is difficult to identify the point at issue. Was it that Ruse dared to criticize Dawkins, an act of *lèse majesté*? Or was it that he even more daringly suggested that science and religion might learn from each other—

which some fanatics, I fear, would regard as an act of treason?

Dawkins here cites approvingly the Chicago geneticist Jerry Coyne, who declared that "the *real* war is between rationalism and superstition. Science is but one form of rationalism, while religion is the most common form of superstition."[24] And so the world is divided into two camps—rationalism and superstition. Just as religions distinguish the saved from the damned, Dawkins shows the same absolute dichotomous mode of thought. It is either black or white; there are no shades of gray. Poor Michael Ruse. Having attacked one bunch of fundamentalists, he finds himself ostracised by another—declared to be intellectually unclean by his erstwhile colleagues.

Dawkins is clearly entrenched in his own peculiar version of a fundamentalist dualism. Yet many will feel that a reality check is appropriate, if not long overdue, here. Dawkins seems to view things from within a highly polarized worldview that is no less apocalyptic and warped than that of the religious fundamentalisms he wishes to eradicate. Is the solution to religious fundamentalism *really* for atheists to replicate its vices? We are offered an atheist fundamentalism that is as deeply flawed and skewed as its religious counterparts.[25] There are better ways to deal with religious fundamentalism. Dawkins is part of the problem here, not its solution.

A CLASH OF FUNDAMENTALISMS

One of the greatest disservices that Dawkins has done to the natural sciences is to portray them as relentlessly and inexorably atheistic. They are nothing of the sort; yet Dawkins's crusading vigor has led to the growth of this alienating perception in many parts of North American conservative Protestantism. Is there any better way to ensure that the sciences are seen in a negative light within this community, as interest in and commitment to religion resurges throughout much of the world? Little wonder that many Darwinians have expressed alarm at this attempt to brand the outlook as atheist. They are being discredited in the eyes of a vast constituency—needlessly and recklessly.

I have already criticized the intelligent design movement, a conservative Christian anti-evolutionary movement whose ideas are also lambasted in *The God Delusion*.[26] Yet ironically, this movement now regards Dawkins as one of its greatest assets. Why? Because his hysterical and dogmatic insistence on the atheist implications of Darwinism is alienating many potential supporters of the theory of evolution. William Dembski, the intellectual architect of this movement, constantly thanks his intelligent Designer for Dawkins.[27] As he put it recently in a somewhat sarcastic e-mail to Dawkins: "I regularly tell my colleagues that you and your work are one of God's greatest gifts to the intelligent-design movement. So please, keep at it!" I suspect that he's delighted by *The God Delusion*.[28]

Small wonder that Ruse (who describes himself as a "hard-line Darwinian") commented in a leaked e-mail to Daniel Dennett that he (Dennett) and Dawkins were "absolute disasters in the fight against intelligent design."

What we need is not knee-jerk atheism but serious grappling with the issues—neither of you are willing to study Christianity seriously and to engage with the ideas—it is just plain silly and grotesquely immoral to claim that Christianity is simply a force for evil, as Richard [Dawkins] claims—more than this, we are in a fight, and we need to make allies in the fight, not simply alienate everyone of good will.[29]

Aha! *Now* we understand why Dawkins has cast Ruse into outer darkness. Don't worry, Michael—you're in good company.

But before his expulsion from Dawkins's Garden of Eden, Ruse had made another telling point. On October 22, 1996, Pope John Paul II issued a statement to the Pontifical Academy of Sciences offering support for the general notion of biological evolution, while criticizing certain materialist interpretations of the idea.[30] (Roman Catholicism, by the way, has never had the difficulties with the notion of evolution that are characteristic of conservative Protestantism.) The pope's statement was welcomed by many scientists. But not Richard Dawkins. Here is Ruse's comment on what happened next: "When John Paul II wrote a letter endorsing Darwinism, Richard Dawkins' response was simply that the pope was a hypocrite, that he could not be genuine about science and that Dawkins himself simply preferred an honest fundamentalist."[31]

Ruse's comment immediately helps us understand what is going on. If Dawkins's agenda was to encourage Christians to accept biological evolution, this statement would have been welcomed. But it's not. Dawkins is totally unable to accept that the pope—or presumably any Christian—could accept evolution. So he is not telling the truth, is he? He can't be. The pope, according to Dawkins, is a superstitious person who is just *pretending* to be rational. It's hard not to believe that science—or rather, a highly contentious and unrepresentative account of science—is here being abused as a weapon to destroy religion.

One of the most melancholy aspects of *The God Delusion* is how its author appears to have made the transition from a scientist with a passionate concern for truth to a crude antireligious propagandist who shows a disregard for evidence. This was evident in the TV series *The Root of All Evil?* which served as a pilot for *The God Delusion*. Here, Dawkins sought out religious extremists who advocated violence in the name of religion, or who were aggressively antiscientific in their outlook. No representative figures were included or considered. Dawkins's conclusion? Religion leads to violence and is antiscience.

Unsurprisingly, the series was panned by its critics, who saw it as intellectually risible. As one senior atheist scientific colleague at Oxford said to me afterward, "Don't judge the rest of us by this pseudointellectual drivel." Yet *The God Delusion* simply continues this flagrantly biased approach to evidence, mocking and excoriating alternatives, refusing to take them seriously. Yes, there are religious people who are deeply hostile to science. And that number will, if anything, simply increase due to Dawkins's polemical use of science in his epic struggle against religion. Perhaps it's time that the scientific community as a whole protested against the abuse of their ideas in the service of such an atheist fundamentalism.

3

What Are the Origins of Religion?

THE CORE, INCONTROVERTIBLE, FOUNDATIONAL ASSUMPTION of atheism is that there is no God. So why would anyone believe in God? For Dawkins this is an utterly irrational belief—like believing in a teapot orbiting the sun.[1] Sure, this is a flawed analogy. Nobody I know believes such nonsense. But that's what Dawkins wants his readers to think—that believing in God is on the same level as cosmic teapots. It's yet another recycled analogy that is all part of his general strategy of systematically mocking, misrepresenting and demonizing competing worldviews, which are always presented in the most naive light possible.

So what new insights does Dawkins have to offer? The best way of understanding Dawkins's approach to the origins of religion is

to see him as taking a traditional atheist proof for the nonexistence
of God and developing it in a new way. It all goes back to Ludwig
Feuerbach, a radical German philosopher who disliked religion.
In 1841, Feuerbach argued that God was basically an invention,
dreamed up by human beings to provide metaphysical and spiritual consolation.[2] His argument runs like this.

> There is no God.
> But lots of people believe in God. Why?
> *Because they want consolation.*
> So they "project" or "objectify" their longings and call this
>   "God."
> So this nonexistent God is simply the projection of human
>   longings.

It's a fascinating argument and has had a deep impact on Western culture. It has its problems, however. For a start, wanting
something is no demonstration that it does not exist. Human thirst
points to the need for water. It also suggests that all worldviews are
a response to human needs and desires—including, of course,
atheism, which can be seen as a response to the human desire for
moral autonomy.

Let's look at two variants, each profoundly relevant to our
theme. One locates the origins of belief in God in sociological factors, the other in psychological factors. Karl Marx argued that the
reason people needed the delusion of God was that they were socially and economically alienated. When the socialist revolution
came there would be no need for religion. It would just die out,
naturally. Which is just as well, as it is a serious obstacle to human

progress. Sigmund Freud argued that the origins of belief in God lay in the longing for a father figure. Once it is appreciated that God is a "wish fulfillment" conjured up as a result of human projection, we can move beyond this infantile illusion and grow up.[3]

Dawkins also offers a naturalist explanation of religion—in this case, one that is highly contrived and unpersuasive. Belief in God might be a byproduct of some other evolutionary mechanism. Here he moves into territory explored by fellow atheist Daniel Dennett in his recent book *Breaking the Spell*.[4] Yet both Dawkins and Dennett adopt a very cognitive view of religion, defining it virtually exclusively in terms of "belief in God." Yet this is certainly not the sole aspect of religion; nor is it even necessarily the most fundamental. A more reliable description of religion would make reference to its many aspects, including knowledge, beliefs, experience, ritual practices, social affiliation, motivation and behavioral consequences.[5]

Despite offering a somewhat attenuated account of religion, Dennett argues that its defining characteristic of belief in God might have evolved for a number of reasons. For instance, we might have a "god center" in our brains. Such a center might depend on a "mystical gene" that was favored by natural selection because people with it tend to survive better. Or religious ideas "could have spread from individual superstitions via shamanism and the early 'wild' strains of religion."

Dawkins adds to such speculations, suggesting that essentially natural tendencies may have become misdirected, ending up as something fundamentally religious. Religion is thus an "accidental by-product" or a "misfiring of something useful."[6] Yet this seems more than a little inconsistent with his own "universal Darwinism," which eschews any notion of purpose—a view famously summarized in his statement that the universe has "no design, no purpose, no evil and no good, nothing but blind pitiless indifference."[7] How can Dawkins speak of religion as something "accidental" when his understanding of the evolutionary process precludes any theoretical framework that allows him to suggest that some outcomes are intentional and others accidental? It is inconsistent with a Darwinian view of the world. For Darwinism, everything is accidental. Things may have the *appearance* of design—but this appearance of design or intentionality arises from random developments. That, after all, was the nub of Dawkins's critique of Paley in *The Blind Watchmaker*.

Yet this is a minor point. The main criticism of this accidental-byproduct theory is the lack of serious evidence offered on its behalf. Where's the *science?* What's the evidence for such a belief? We find speculation and supposition taking the place of the rigorous evidence-driven and evidence-based arguments that we have a right to expect. Dawkins's theories of the biological origins of religion, though interesting, must be considered to be highly speculative. His arguments about the psychological origins of religion are littered with "maybes" and "mights," verbal signposts that there is no substantial evidence for the highly tenuous and speculative ideas he explores with his readers.

On reading this section, I felt that I was being bludgeoned into submission to his ideas by the sheer force of his assertions rather than led along willingly on account of the weight of the evidence on the one hand and Dawkins's skill in presenting it on the other.

The arguments begin with cautious "could be" statements, advancing tentative hypotheses for consideration. Yet they rapidly become bold "is" statements, making assertions without the firm evidence normally thought to be required for rigorous scientific argument.

I would place Dawkins (and Dennett) in the broad tradition of naturalist explanation of religion that includes Feuerbach, Marx and Freud. Whatever the benefits of religions might be, these writers believe that they arise entirely inside human minds. No spiritual realities exist outside us. Natural explanations may be given of the origins of belief in God. In the end, this is a circular argument, which presupposes its conclusions. It begins from the assumption that there is no God and then proceeds to show that an explanation of God can be offered which is entirely consistent with this. In fact, it is basically an atheist reworking of Thomas Aquinas's "Five Ways," arguing that a consistent account of things may be offered without being obliged to propose the existence of God.

At an early stage in *The God Delusion,* Dawkins represents atheism as the ultimate outcome of a process of whittling down irrational beliefs about the supernatural.[8] You begin with polytheism—believing in lots of gods. Then as time progresses and your thinking becomes more sophisticated, you move on to monotheism—belief in only one God. Atheism just takes this one step further. As Dawkins playfully remarks, it just involves believing in one less god than before. It's the obvious next step in the progress of religion. Yet the history of religion obliges us to speak about the diversification, not the progression, of religion. The evidence simply isn't there to allow us to speak about any kind of natural progression from polytheism to monotheism—and thence to atheism.[9]

Yet there is a much deeper question here, one that Dawkins does not even begin to address. *What is the difference between a worldview and a religion?* The dividing line is notoriously imprecise and, many would say, is constructed by those with vested interests to defend. A worldview is a comprehensive way of viewing reality that tries to make sense of its various elements within a single, overarching way of looking at things. Some, of course, are religious; many are not. Buddhism, existentialism, Islam, atheism and Marxism all fall into this category. Some worldviews claim to be universally true; others, more in tune with the postmodern ethos, view themselves as local. None of them can be "proved" to be right. Precisely because they represent "big picture" ways of engaging with the world, their fundamental beliefs ultimately lie beyond final proof.

And here is the point: worldviews can easily promote fanaticism. Dawkins treats this as a defining characteristic of religion, airbrushing out of his account of violence any suggestion that it might be the result of political fanaticism—or even atheism. He is adamant that he himself, as a good atheist, would never fly airplanes into skyscrapers or commit any other outrageous act of violence or oppression. Good for him. Neither would I. Yet there are those in *both* our constituencies who would. Dawkins and I may both disavow violence and urge all within our groups to do so. But the harsh reality is that religious and antireligious violence has happened, and is likely to continue to do so. So important is this point that we shall deal with it in greater detail later.

Dawkins stands in the naturalist tradition that aims to explain the origins of religion without invoking the existence or activity of a god. Like Freud before him, Dawkins sets out to demonstrate that all aspects of religion may be accounted for in terms of a single theory—in this case, "universal Darwinism."[10] In undertaking such an ambitious project, he has many intellectual hurdles to overcome. In this chapter, we shall consider whether his approach matches up to the rigorous evidential demands that are demanded by the natural sciences.

DEFINING RELIGION

A clear definition of precisely what is being studied is essential to the serious scientific study of any entity or phenomenon. The failure of past attempts to offer a reliable and warranted definition of *religion* is widely conceded in the vast scholarly literature devoted to this subject. Of the myriad of definitions of religion offered over the last 150 years, each of which presented itself as being scientific or objective, none has been sufficiently resilient or representative to command continuing support.[11] Furthermore, definitions of religion are rarely neutral but are often generated to favor beliefs and institutions with which one is in sympathy and penalize those to which one is hostile, often reflecting little more than the "particular purposes and prejudices of individual scholars."[12]

Dawkins deals with this serious problem by evading it, choosing not to engage with the issues that have famously destroyed previous attempts to generalize about the roots of religion. His analysis rests on the "general principles" of religion[13] he finds in James Frazer's *Golden Bough*—a highly impressionistic early work of anthropology first published in 1890.[14] It is a highly puzzling strategy. Why on earth should Dawkins's theory of the roots of religion depend so heavily on the core assumptions of a work that is well over a century old and now largely discredited?

The rise of modern anthropology can be seen as a direct reaction to the manifest failures of Frazer's *Golden Bough*. What were those failings? First, it adopted what can only be described as an imperialist attitude to the cultural context of religion in order to generate universal explanatory concepts. Second, it totally lacked any serious basis in systematic empirical study. Dawkins seems to repeat both these errors, drawing ambitious theories about the origins of faith without any serious attempt to engage representatively with the large body of scholarly literature that reports and assesses the empirical evidence since Frazer, and instead making highly questionable generalized assertions about the nature of religion.

So why does Dawkins want to follow Frazer in reducing religion to some single universal trait, neglecting the mass of research that suggests it is much more complex and diverse, incapable of being forced into a simple set of universal beliefs or attitudes? The answer is clear: because by doing so, he believes it can be analyzed within the "universal Darwinism" that represents his core belief system. "Universal features of a species demand a Darwinian explanation."[15]

But that's precisely the problem: it is now known that religion does *not* exhibit the "universal features" that Dawkins's preferred approach demands, and that late Victorian works of the anthropology of religion erroneously regarded as axiomatic. It is one of the many points at which *The God Delusion* depends on discarded nineteenth-century assumptions to make a twenty-first-century

case against religion. Dawkins tends to evade this point by direct-
ing his criticisms against the three great monotheistic religions.
But, first, these represent only three of many global religious par-
adigms; second, there are highly significant differences between
the three (one obvious example: Christianity does not demand ritual food practices or customs such as kosher or *halal*); and third,
there are huge differences within individual religions (compare
traditional Roman Catholic Christianity with evangelical or Pente-
costal Christianity).

Even more worrying, Frazer's strategic assumption of "the essential similarity of man's chief wants everywhere and at all times"
leads Dawkins to offer an account of the origins of religion based
on an alleged "universal tendency to let belief be coloured by desire." It is a theory that can be traced back to Ludwig Feuerbach
and Sigmund Freud. Neither these seminal thinkers nor their
many critics are mentioned, let alone engaged in defense of such
an ambitious proposal. Dawkins's authority at this point? William
Shakespeare.

Dawkins identifies "wish fulfilment" as a global feature of religion. Now, there is a grain of truth in his analysis. The way human
beings perceive the world is indeed colored by our agendas and
expectations. "Cognitive bias" is indeed a fundamental characteristic of human psychology.[16] Yet in general this unconscious bias
is manifested not so much in our believing what we would like to
be true as in maintaining the status quo of our beliefs. The driving
force is not wishful thinking but conservative thinking—that is,
thinking that conserves an existing worldview.

For example, many people have a positive view of themselves, a sense that the universe is benevolent and that other people like them. They maintain this view by attending to data that fits this view and minimizing that which does not. Others (such as depressed or traumatized people) see themselves as worthless, view the universe as malevolent and think others are out to get them. Once more, they discount or minimize the significance of any data that does not fit in with this view.

We thus have a built-in resistance to change our position—a resistance that is underpinned by cognitive biases that predispose us to fail to notice or to discount data that are inconsistent with our view. On the whole we do this because it is efficient—it takes effort and is upsetting to have to change one's mind—even if the change is in a positive direction. *The God Delusion* is a wonderful case study of exactly this kind of unconscious bias. Without full awareness that he is doing so, Dawkins foregrounds evidence that fits his own views and discounts or distorts evidence that does not.

While cognitive bias helps us cope with a complex world, there are some situations where it is very important to minimize its effects. Scientific investigation is one of these. The entire point of the scientific method is to reduce, and where possible eliminate, such bias, to strive to give as objective and fair an account as possible. Dawkins does not apply this method to his consideration of religion.

Do cognitive biases play a part in religious belief? The evidence is that they are as important here as in any other area of life. An understanding of this aspect of cognitive processing may well shed light on the conservatism of established religion—the factors that maintain it in the face of threat.[17] But they are less important in

understanding the origins of religion and new religious move-
ments, which are characterized by *opposition* to the status quo
rather than conservatism.

BELIEF IN GOD AND RELIGION

How are belief in God and religion related? Dawkins fails to make
this critical distinction, seeing "religion" and "belief in God" as little more than two sides of the same coin. This inadequate approach does not even begin to deal with the problem of nontheis-
tic religion, an issue which is dismissed with little more than a
curt, soon forgotten acknowledgment.

The God Delusion tends to limit its engagement with religion to
demonstrating that its ideas are ridiculous or pernicious, violating
the integrity of the human mind or contaminating the purity of the
human heart. Yet this emphasis on ideas and rituals leads to a
somewhat restricted account of religion, which fails to do justice
to its many levels of meaning. Any account or description of religion would also have to include at the very least knowledge, experience, group affiliation, motivation and ethical consequences.[18]

Dawkins wants to offer a Darwinian explanation of religion. So
is he accounting for belief in God? Or for religiosity? Or both?
There are many who believe passionately in God but eschew religious behavior—evangelicals represent a case in point. Again, it is
possible to have religious attitudes without any attending belief in
God—Buddhism is a case in point. Many individuals have a rev-
erential attitude toward nature that is not ultimately theistic but
could still reasonably be termed *religious*.

The fundamental argument here is that religion is (though

Dawkins does not use this term) an epiphenomenon—a random byproduct of something else that has selective advantage. But in order to pursue this line with any rigor, it is vital to define what aspect of religion is being considered. Dawkins refers to "beliefs," and by this he appears to mean something corresponding to creedal statements, such as "belief in the existence of the Trinity." This is a simplistic approach to an area that is much more complex than it might appear on superficial inspection.

The type of belief that might usefully be subjected to his sort of Darwinian explanation are what are sometimes referred to as "hot cognitions," such as "God likes me" or "I am a sinner," that express felt meaning, rather than propositional statements such as "God is good" or "Jesus' mother was a virgin." The psychological processing systems involved in these two different types of statements are quite different in their characteristics and likely to fulfill distinct psychological functions. The compelling nature of religious faith almost certainly relates to processing by what psychologists John Teasdale and Philip Barnard refer to as the "implicational" subsystem rather than the "propositional" subsystem.[19] This is an emerging field that requires careful analysis and does not seem to fit easily into Dawkins's exclusively propositional account of religious belief that focuses on dogmas.

Dogmas are not only propositional; they arise in a social context and fulfill a social function. For instance, Christian dogmas define agreed community "belief statements," which emerged after extended periods of reflection on the fundamental resources and experiences of the Christian community.[20] They can be thought of as group identity markers, consensual social constructs that try to systematize religious experience and individual beliefs. They survive in part for reasons of affiliation and conservatism, and partly because they express indirectly something that may be of more fundamental importance.

Psychologists of religion are only just beginning to come to grips with this important distinction—trying to identify personal "hot cognitions" rather than affiliative group statements that may be assented to but may not be *felt* to be true.[21] People may be prepared to assent to propositional contradictions (renaming them "paradoxes") and counterfactual belief statements (renaming them "mysteries") precisely because the cognitive processing associated with their personal religion is not taking place at this level at all but at an intuitive level that is not easily amenable to description in propositional terms.

More work clearly needs to be done on defining and describing the nature of religious belief. A failure to offer a defensible definition of religion ultimately negates Dawkins's attempts to offer a Darwinian account of its origins. Nevertheless, one issue he raises in exploring the question should be noted.[22] Dawkins argues that human beings are psychologically primed for religion because the psychological processes that predispose us to religion (however defined) confer selective advantage in other areas of life. Religion has no selective advantage in its own right. It is an epiphenomenon—and a socially and psychologically dysfunctional one at that.

So are we psychologically primed for religion? This is an important question, and it clearly requires a psychological answer. It soon becomes clear that Dawkins is not qualified to give one. Dawkins shows himself to be ill at ease with psychology and neuroscience, despite the critical importance they play at this juncture in his argument. For example, his assertions that the brain is a "collection of organs (or 'modules')" for doing various cognitive functions, and that religion "is a by-product of the misfiring of several of these modules"[23] is muddled—conflating the language of information processing and brain physiology.[24] Elsewhere he seems to confuse brain mechanisms with psychological constructs.[25] This isn't the brilliant popularization of difficult scientific ideas that we saw in *The Selfish Gene;* it's just a confused and misleading account of someone else's area of specialization.

In his discussion of brain activity as a possible cause of religion, Dawkins might have cared to recognize that this activity is actually the cause (in the sense of being a necessary condition) of *all* human experience and behavior—including his own.[26] There is nothing specific to religion here. More seriously, he draws attention to the hypothesis of Michael Persinger that religious experience is associated with pathological brain activity, subtly implying that religion is itself therefore pathological.[27] Readers ought to be aware (for Dawkins does not mention it) that Persinger's experiments have been severely criticized for their conceptual and design limitations, and that his theory is no longer regarded as plausible.[28]

The problem that Dawkins confronts in offering a psychological account of the origins of religion can be stated like this. It is certainly possible to argue that some aspects of human cognitive processes may help explain how religious ideas are generated or sustained. Yet as the psychologist Fraser Watts points out, it is necessary to recognize a multiplicity of causes in such areas. Some scientists have fallen into the habit of asking, What caused

A? Was it X or Y? But in the human sciences, multiple causes are the norm. For example, consider the question, Is depression caused by physical *or* social factors? The answer is that it is caused by both. As Watts points out, the history of such research "ought to make us wary of asking whether an apparent revelation of God really is such, or whether is has some other natural explanation, in terms of people's thought processes or brain processes."[29] To put it crudely, God, human brain processes and psychological processes may all be causal factors in human religious experience. Dawkins himself uses the example of romantic love.[30] The experience of romantic love may be said to be caused by the words and actions of one's lover, the sense one makes of them and activity in those areas of the brain particularly concerned with emotional processing. The ultimate cause is the beloved, and it can be argued that whatever the proximal causes the ultimate cause of religious experience is God.

In considering the psychological origins of religion, it is far from clear why Dawkins neglects to engage with Freud. Freud's own heroic but incoherent and ultimately abortive attempts to explain religion in terms of psychopathology illuminate some of the difficulties encountered, as the Belgian psychologist Antoine Vergote has pointed out. Freud rightly saw that religion was the "most complex phenomenon in civilization," making it impossible to explain by any single factor. No individual psychological process could be said to generate the idea of God. Vergote's analysis of Freud's attempts, however, made it clear that "the validity of religious belief can neither be substantiated nor refuted by scientific reasoning."[31]

And in the midst of this interesting and potentially important argument, Dawkins reintroduces two of the most unpersuasive, pseudoscientific ideas to have made their appearance in discussions of the roots of religion in recent years—the idea of God as a "virus of the mind" and the "meme." An already faltering argument is simply given the kiss of death by the recycling of these implausible notions, which fail to command assent within the mainline scientific community. In what follows, we shall look at both of these.

THE VIRUS OF THE MIND

Every now and then, highly entrepreneurial individuals develop new ideas or concepts that they believe offer better explanations of the observational evidence than those of their rivals. Some—such as the electron and gene—find acceptance within the scientific community and become part of its received wisdom. Others wither and die simply because they are found to be of little use, explanatorily redundant or inadequately grounded in experiment. "Phlogiston" and "caloric" are examples of these defunct concepts, now relegated to textbooks of the history of science as interesting mistakes.

The same must be said of the two notions that we are about to explore—the idea of the "virus of the mind" and the "meme." Neither has made it into the annals of scientific orthodoxy. Both hover on the fringes, defended chiefly on account of their antireligious potential (which is easily overstated) rather than their evidential foundations.

Of these two, the more implausible is the notion of a "virus of the mind." During the 1990s, Dawkins introduced the idea of God as some kind of mental virus that infected otherwise healthy minds. It was a powerful image that appealed to a growing public awareness of the risk of physical infections from HIV and software infections from computer viruses. Viruses were nasty and destructive—precisely the message that Dawkins wished to convey about belief in God.

Since belief in God is utterly irrational (one of Dawkins's core beliefs), there has to be some way of explaining why so many people—in fact, by far the greater part of the world's population—fall victim to such a delusion. Dawkins argues that it is like being infected with a contagious virus that spreads throughout entire populations. Yet the analogy—belief in God is *like* a virus—seems to then assume ontological substance: Belief in God *is* a virus of the mind. Yet biological viruses are not merely hypothesized; they can be identified, observed and their structure and mode of operation determined. Yet this hypothetical "virus of the mind" is an essentially polemical construction, devised to discredit ideas that Dawkins does not like.

So are all ideas viruses of the mind? Dawkins draws an absolute distinction between rational, scientific and evidence-based ideas and spurious, irrational notions—such as religious beliefs. The latter, not the former, count as mental viruses. But who decides what is "rational" and "scientific"? Dawkins does not see this as a problem, believing that he can easily categorize such ideas, separating the sheep from the goats.

Except it all turns out to be horribly complicated, losing the simplicity and elegance that marks a great idea. For instance, every worldview—religious or secular—ends up falling into the category of "belief systems" precisely because it cannot be proved.

That is simply the nature of worldviews, and everyone knows it. It prevents nobody from holding a worldview in the first place and doing so with complete intellectual integrity in the second. In the end, Dawkins's idea simply implodes, falling victim to his own subjective judgment of what is rational and true. It's not an idea that is taken seriously within the scientific community, and it can safely be disregarded.

I was severely and quite properly critical of this pseudoscientific idea in *Dawkins' God,* noting that it lacked any basis in evidence and seemed to depend on Dawkins's highly subjective personal judgment as to what was rational or not.[32] This discredited idea now seems to have a purely walk-on part in the narrative of *The God Delusion,* which alludes to a 1993 article in which Dawkins wrote about God as a "virus of the mind."[33] It's clearly about to be written out of the plot altogether, and not too soon. Its passing will not be mourned.

LONG LIVE THE MEME!

The meme is much the more interesting idea and plays a significant role in Dawkins's attempt to devise a plausible account of the roots of religion. His appeal to the meme occurs late in his discussion of the roots of religion, by which time his argument had become so contrived and unpersuasive that it stood in need of redemption.[34] Dawkins defends the idea with a proprietorial intensity, as well he might—after all, he invented it. Maybe that's why he titled the section "Tread Softly, Because You Tread on My Memes."

Dawkins first introduced the idea back in 1976, toward the end of his *Selfish Gene.* In my view, this is one of his best books:

his scientific analysis is bold and original; his capacity to communicate is evident for all to see; and his emerging antireligious bias is kept under a tight leash. It's a million miles from the unscientific antireligious ranting of *The God Delusion*. The argument is that there exists a fundamental analogy between biological and cultural evolution: both involve a replicator. In the case of biological evolution, this replicator is the gene; in the case of cultural evolution it's a hypothesized entity, which Dawkins termed a *meme*. In an image-rich passage, he spoke of these memes "leaping from brain to brain."

For Dawkins the idea of God is perhaps the supreme example of such a meme. Dawkins dogmatically insists that religious belief is "blind trust," which refuses to take due account of evidence or subject itself to examination. So why do people believe in God when there is no God to believe in? The proposed answer lies in the ability of a "God-meme" to replicate itself in the human mind. The God meme performs particularly well because it has "high survival value, or infective power, in the environment provided by human culture."[35] People do not believe in God because they have given long and careful thought to the matter; they do so because they have been infected by a powerful meme, which has "leapt" into their brains.[36]

Yet has anyone actually seen these things, whether leaping from brain to brain or just hanging out? The issue, it must be noted, has nothing to do with religion. It is whether the meme can be considered to be a viable scientific hypothesis when there is no clear operational definition of a meme, no testable model for how memes influence culture and why standard selection models are not adequate, a general tendency to ignore the sophisticated social science models of information transfer already in place, and a high degree of circularity in the explanation of the power of memes.[37]

The meme is essentially a biological notion, arising from Dawkins's core belief in "universal Darwinism," which leads him to discount economic, cultural or learning-theory accounts of religion. But why should biology be able to explain culture? Isn't this actually the area of study of cultural and intellectual historians, not to mention social anthropologists? Maurice Bloch, professor of anthropology at the London School of Economics, is representative of the "exasperated reaction of many anthropologists to the general idea of memes." The meme is a biological answer to an anthropological problem, which simply disregards and discounts the major successes of the discipline of anthropology in the explanation of cultural development—which took place without needing to bother with the unsubstantiated idea of a meme.[38] The meme is conceptually redundant. The alternative models of cultural evolution developed within the scientific discipline dedicated to precisely this area of investigation are conveniently overlooked by those evolutionary biologists wishing to extend the competency of their discipline from the biological to the cultural.[39]

In *The God Delusion,* Dawkins sets out the idea of memes as if it were established scientific orthodoxy, making no mention of the inconvenient fact that the mainstream scientific community views it as a decidedly flaky idea, best relegated to the margins. The meme is presented as if it were an actually existing entity, with huge potential to explain the origins of religion. Dawkins is even able to develop an advanced vocabulary based on his own convictions—such as *memeplex.*

So why are the arguments of leading critics of memetics within the scientific community not identified and their highly significant criticisms confronted, fairly and squarely, point by point? It would, of course, have made Dawkins's bold assertions about the "memetic" origins of religion seem rather misplaced. It is clear that before we get around to talking about whether these alleged memes have any relevance to explaining the origins of religion, they need to be demonstrated as scientifically necessary. And the science just isn't there.

Take one of Dawkins's characteristically bold statements: "memes can sometimes display very high fidelity."[40] This is a creedal statement posing as a statement of scientific fact. Dawkins is virulently critical of Christians who say things like "God is faithful." Yet in this statement, he makes precisely the error of which he accuses others. He is translating an observation into his own theoretical language, which is not spoken elsewhere within the scientific community. The *observation* is that ideas can be passed from one individual, group or generation to another; Dawkins's *theoretical interpretation* of this observation—which is here presented simply as fact—involves attributing fidelity to what most regard as being a nonexistent entity.

Dawkins, in my view, makes his critique of religion dependent on a hypothetical, unobserved entity that can be dispensed with completely in order to make sense of what we observe. But isn't that actually a core atheist critique of God—that God is an unobserved hypothesis which can be dispensed with easily? The scientific evidence for memes is actually much weaker than the historical evidence for the existence of Jesus—something that Dawkins revealingly regards as open to question, while doggedly defending memes.[41] And since the evidence for memes is so tenuous, do we have to propose a meme for believing in memes in the first place?[42]

But Dawkins might respond that the alleged failure of his quest to show that the origins of religion are purely natural is actually of little importance. Who cares about how the roots of religion are to be explained when it is so manifestly evil in practice? We must therefore turn to consider whether religion is indeed, as Dawkins would have us believe, the axis of evil that threatens to plunge civilization into a new dark age.

4

Is Religion Evil?

RELIGION IS EVIL! WHEN IT IS BANISHED FROM THE FACE of the earth, we can live in peace! It is a familiar theme. The God that Dawkins does not believe in is "a petty, unjust, unforgiving control freak; a vindictive, bloodthirsty ethnic cleanser; a misogynistic, homophobic, racist, infanticidal, genocidal, filicidal, pestilential, megalomaniacal, sadomasochistic, capriciously malevolent bully."[1] Come to think of it, I don't believe in a God like that either. In fact, I don't know anybody who does.

Dawkins at least has the graciousness to appreciate this point. The God whom I know and love is described by Dawkins as "insipid," summed up in the "mawkishly nauseating" idea of "Gentle Jesus, meek and mild." While some readers will take offense at this description, it is the probably the mildest criticism of religion of-fered anywhere in his book.

RELIGION LEADS TO VIOLENCE

Dawkins is, I think, entirely right when he exposes and challenges religious violence. I am with him totally and hope that the force of his point here will not be obscured by the inaccuracy of much of the remainder of *The God Delusion*. It is clear that his ire is directed primarily against Islamic fundamentalism, particularly its *jihadist* forms.[2] All of us need to work to rid the world of the baleful influ-ence of religious violence. On that point Dawkins and I are agreed.

Yet is this a *necessary* feature of religion? Here, I must insist that we abandon the outmoded idea that all religions say more or less the same things. They clearly do not. I write as a Christian who holds that the face, will and character of God are fully disclosed in Jesus of Nazareth. And as Dawkins knows, Jesus of Nazareth did no violence to anyone. He was the object, not the agent, of vio-lence. Instead of meeting violence with violence, rage with rage, Christians are asked to "turn the other cheek," and not to let the sun go down on their anger. This is about the elimination of the roots of violence—no, more than that: it is about its *transfiguration*.

The importance of this ethic can be seen in a tragic event in North America that took place in October 2006, within a week of the publication of *The God Delusion*. Interestingly, the episode il-lustrates both the negative and positive sides of religion. A gun-man with some kind of religious grudge (he was "angry with God") broke into an Amish school in Pennsylvania and gunned down a group of schoolgirls. Five of the young girls died. The Amish are a Protestant religious group who repudiate any form of violence on account of their understanding of the moral authority of the person and teaching of Jesus of Nazareth. When those unfortunate schoolchildren were murdered, the Amish community urged forgiveness. There would be no violence, no revenge—only the offering of forgiveness. The gunman's widow spoke, gratefully and movingly, of how this provided the "healing" that she and her three children "so desperately needed."

Dawkins is condescending about the Amish. Yet I cannot help but feel that he misses something rather important in his blanket dismissal of their significance. If the world was more like Jesus of Nazareth, violence might indeed be a thing of the past. But that does not appear to be an answer that Dawkins feels comfortable with.[3]

As someone who grew up in Northern Ireland, I know only too well about religious violence. There is no doubt that religion can generate violence. But it's not alone in this. The history of the twentieth century has given us a frightening awareness of how political extremism can equally cause violence. In Latin America millions of people seem to have "disappeared" as a result of ruthless campaigns of violence by right-wing politicians and their militias. In Cambodia, Pol Pot eliminated his millions in the name of socialism.[4]

The rise of the Soviet Union was of particular significance. Lenin regarded the elimination of religion as central to the socialist revolution, and he put in place measures designed to eradicate religious beliefs through the "protracted use of violence." One of the greatest tragedies of this dark era in human history was that those who sought to eliminate religious belief through violence and oppression believed they were justified in doing so. They were accountable to no higher authority than the state.

In one of his more bizarre creedal statements as an atheist, Dawkins insists that there is "not the smallest evidence" that atheism systematically influences people to do bad things. It's an astonishing, naive and somewhat sad statement. Dawkins is clearly an ivory-tower atheist, disconnected from the real and brutal world of the twentieth century. The facts are otherwise. In their efforts to enforce their atheist ideology, the Soviet authorities systematically destroyed and eliminated the vast majority of churches and priests during the period 1918-1941.[5] The statistics make for dreadful reading. This violence and repression was undertaken in pursuit of an atheist agenda—the elimination of religion.

This hardly fits in with another of Dawkins's creedal statements: "*I do not believe* there is an atheist in the world who would bulldoze Mecca—or Chartres, York Minster, or Notre Dame."[6] Sadly, this noble sentiment is a statement about his personal credulity, not the reality of things. The history of the Soviet Union is replete with the burning and dynamiting of huge numbers of churches. His pleading that atheism is innocent of the violence and oppression that he associates with religion is simply untenable, and suggests a significant blind spot.

Dawkins's naive view that atheists would never carry out crimes in the name of atheism simply founders on the cruel rocks of reality. One example will suffice. In his outstanding study of the Romanian Christian dissident intellectual Petre Tutea (1902-1991), the Oxford scholar Alexandru Popescu documents the physical and mental degradation Tutea suffered as part

of systematic persecution of religion in Romania during the Soviet era until the downfall and execution of Nicolae Ceausescu.[7]
During this period, Tutea spent thirteen years as a prisoner of
conscience and twenty-eight years under house arrest. His personal story is enormously illuminating for those who want to understand the power of religious faith to console and maintain
personal identity under precisely the forms of persecution that
Dawkins believes do not exist.

Dawkins is simply in denial about the darker side of atheism,
making him a less than credible critic of religion. He has a fervent,
unquestioning faith in the universal goodness of atheism, which
he refuses to subject to critical examination. Yes, there is much
that is wrong with contemporary religion and much that needs to
be reformed. Yet the same is also true of atheism, which needs to
subject itself to the self-searching intellectual and moral criticisms
that religious systems are willing to direct against themselves.

The reality of the situation is that human beings are capable of
both violence and moral excellence—and that both of these may
be provoked by worldviews, whether religious or otherwise. It is
not a comfortable insight, but one that alerts us to the shortcom-
ings and dangers of identifying any one people group as the source
of violence and the ills of humanity. It may facilitate scapegoating;
it hardly advances the cause of civilization.

THE HUMAN ABUSE OF IDEALS

Dawkins would, I think, protest that religious worldviews offer
motivations for violence that are not paralleled elsewhere—for example, the thought of entering paradise after a suicidal attack.[8] Yet

this conclusion is a little hasty and poorly argued. *The God Delusion* is to be seen as one of a number of books to emerge from the events now universally referred to as 9/11—the suicide attacks on buildings in Washington and New York.[9] For Dawkins it is obvious that religious belief leads to suicide bombings. It's a view that his less critical secular readers will applaud, provided they haven't read the empirical studies of why people are driven to suicide bombings in the first place.

As Robert Pape showed in his definitive account of the motivations of such attacks, based on surveys of every suicide bombing since 1980, religious belief of any kind is neither necessary nor sufficient to create suicide bombers—despite Dawkins's breezy simplifications.[10] (Remember, the infamous "suicide vest" was invented by the secessionist Tamil Tigers in Sri Lanka back in 1991.) Pape argues is that the fundamental motivation is political: the desire to force the withdrawal of foreign forces occupying land believed to belong to an oppressed people who have seriously limited military resources at their disposal. This isn't what Dawkins will want to hear, but it is an important element in reflecting on how this phenomenon arose and what might need to be done to end it.

Dawkins, however, seems to have a rather different answer. Since religion is the problem, its disappearance will be to the general benefit of civilization. Dawkins, however, seems more than a little coy about just how religion might vanish. There is a serious risk that criticism of a people's religion might be misconstrued to represent (or encourage) hostility toward them *as a social group*. Legitimate criticism of religious ideas can all too easily give way to the rather more disturbing and dangerous vilification of a people.

The real issue is that religion possesses a capacity to transcendentalize normal human conflicts and disagreements, transforming them into cosmic battles of good and evil in which the authority and will of a transcendent reality is implicated. Divine warfare is terrestrialized, its mandate transferred to affairs on earth. When this situation arises, the normal constraints and compromises that allow humanity to solve potentially explosive situations are trumped.[11]

Yet Dawkins fails to appreciate that when a society rejects the idea of God, it tends to transcendentalize alternatives—such as the ideals of liberty or equality. These now become quasi-divine authorities, which none are permitted to challenge. Perhaps the most familiar example of this dates from the French Revolution, at a time when traditional notions of God were discarded as obsolete and replaced by transcendentalized human values.

Madame Rolande was brought to the guillotine to face execution on trumped-up charges in 1792. As she prepared to die, she bowed mockingly toward the statue of liberty in the Place de la Révolution and uttered the words for which she is remembered: "liberty, what crimes are committed in your name." All ideals—divine, transcendent, human or invented—are capable of being abused. That's just the way human nature is. And knowing this, we need to work out what to do about it rather than lashing out uncritically at religion.

Suppose Dawkins's dream were to come true and religion were to disappear. Would that end the divisions within humanity? Certainly not. Such divisions are ultimately social constructs that reflect the fundamental sociological need for communities to self-define and identify those who are "in" and those who are "out," those who are "friends" and those who are "foes." The importance of "binary opposition" in shaping perceptions of identity has been highlighted in recent years, not least on account of the major debate between different schools of critical thought over whether such oppositions determine and shape human thought or are the outcome of human thought. [12] A series of significant "binary oppositions" are held to have shaped Western thought—such as male-female and white-black. This binary opposition leads to the construction of the category of "the other"—the devalued half of a binary opposition, when applied to groups of people. Group identity is often fostered by defining "the other"—as, for example, in Nazi Germany, with its opposition "Aryan-Jew." At times, this binary opposition is defined in religious terms—as in Catholic-Protestant or believer-infidel.

As is well known, the binary opposition Catholic-Protestant came to be perceived as normative within Northern Ireland. Each side saw its opponent as "the other," a perception that was relentlessly reinforced by novelists and other shapers of public opinion. [13] Media reporting of the social unrest in Northern Ireland from 1970 to about 1995 reinforced the plausibility of this judgment. Yet this is a historically conditioned oppositionalism shaped and determined by complex social forces. *It is not a specifically religious phenomenon.* Religion was merely the social demarcator that dominated in this situation. In others, the demarcators would have to do with ethnic or cultural origins, language, gender, age, social class, sexual orientation, wealth, tribal allegiance, ethical values or political views.[14]

This clearly points to religion, at least in theory, as a potential catalyst for rage and violence in some contexts. In concurring, Dawkins makes a significant concession in recognizing the *sociological* origins of division and exclusion. "Religion is a label of in-group/out-group enmity and vendetta, not necessarily worse than other labels such as skin colour, language, or preferred football team, but often available when other labels are not."[15] Yet even here, his antireligious animus leads him to some problematic judgments. To give one very obvious example: vendettas rarely have their origins in religious concerns.[16]

The simplistic belief that the elimination of religion would lead to the ending of violence, social tension or discrimination is thus sociologically naive. It fails to take account of the way in which human beings create values and norms, and make sense of their identity and their surroundings. If religion were to cease to exist, other social demarcators would emerge as decisive, some of which would become transcendentalized in due course. Dawkins has no interest in sociology, as might be expected. Yet the study of how individuals and societies function casts serious doubt on one of the most fundamental assertions of his analysis.

It is well established that prejudice and discrimination are shaped by perception and group identities.[17] Gross simplifications about religion, exclusion and violence will simply delay and defer a solution of humanity's real problems. The question of the future role of religion in the West is far too important to leave to the fanatics or to atheist fundamentalists. There is a real need to deal with the ultimate causes of social division and exclusion. Religion's in there, along with a myriad of other factors. Yes, it can cause problems. But it also has the capacity to transform, creating a deep sense of personal identity and value, and bringing social cohesion.[18] Let's skip the rhetoric and cut to the reality. It's much less simple than Dawkins's stereotypes—but it might actually help us address the real social issues we face in modern Western culture.

JESUS AND LOVING ONE'S NEIGHBOR

A criticism that is often directed against religion is that it encourages the formation and maintenance of in-groups and out-groups. For Dawkins, removing religion is essential if this form of social demarcation and discrimination is to be defeated. But what, many will wonder, about Jesus of Nazareth? Wasn't this a core theme of his teaching—that the love of God transcends and subsequently abrogates such social divisions?

Dawkins's analysis here is unacceptable. There are points at which his ignorance of religion ceases to be amusing and simply becomes risible. In dealing with this question he draws extensively on a paper published in *Skeptic* magazine in 1995 by John Hartung, which asserts that—and here I cite Dawkins's summary:

> Jesus was a devotee of the same in-group morality—coupled with out-group hostility—that was taken for granted in the Old Testament. Jesus was a loyal Jew. It was Paul who invented the idea of taking the Jewish God to the Gentiles. Hartung puts it more bluntly than I dare: "Jesus would have turned over in his grave if he had known that Paul would be taking his plan to the pigs."[19]

Many Christian readers of this will be astonished at this bizarre misrepresentation of things being presented as if it were gospel truth. Yet, I regret to say, it is representative of Dawkins's method: ridicule, distort, belittle and demonize. Still, at least it will give Christian readers an idea of the lack of any scholarly objectivity or basic human sense of fairness that now pervades atheist fundamentalism.

There is little point in arguing with such fundamentalist nonsense. It's about as worthwhile as trying to persuade a flat-earther that the world is actually round. Dawkins seems to be so deeply trapped within his own worldview that he cannot assess alternatives. Yet many readers would value a more reliable and informed response rather than accepting Dawkins's antireligious tirades. Let's look at things as they actually stand.

In the first place, Jesus explicitly extends the Old Testament command to "love your neighbor" to "love your *enemy*" (Matthew 5:44). Far from endorsing out-group hostility, Jesus both commended and commanded an ethic of out-group affirmation. As this feature of the teaching of Jesus of Nazareth is so well-known and distinctive, it is inexcusable that Dawkins should make no mention of it. Christians may certainly be accused of failing to live up to this demand. But it is there, right at the heart of the Christian ethic.[20]

In the second place, many readers would point out that the familiar story of the Good Samaritan (Luke 10) makes it clear that the command to "love your neighbor" extends far beyond Judaism. (Indeed, this aspect of the teaching of Jesus of Nazareth seems to have resulted in people suspecting Jesus of actually being a Samaritan; see John 8:48.) It is certainly true that Jesus, a Palestinian Jew, gave priority to the Jews as God's chosen people, but his definition of who was a "true Jew" was radically broad. It included those who had excluded themselves from Judaism by intimate collaboration with Roman occupying forces. In the New Testament this out-group is variously referred to as "sinners," "tax collectors" and "prostitutes" (for instance Matthew 21:31-32; Luke 15:1-2). One of the main charges leveled against Jesus by his critics within Judaism was his open acceptance of these out-groups. Indeed a substantial part of his teaching can be seen as a defense of his behavior toward them.[21] Jesus' welcome of marginalized groups who inhabited an ambiguous position between "in" and "out" is also well attested in accounts of his willingness to touch those considered by his culture to be ritually unclean (for instance Matthew 8:3; 9:20-25).

Jesus' attitude to Greco-Roman Gentiles as recounted in the Gospels is more cautious and ambivalent. In both accounts of the healing of such people by Jesus (Matthew 8:5-13; 15:22-28) he is described as being open to persuasion and as both surprised and learning something from the encounter. (Yes—contrary to what Dawkins assumes, orthodox Christianity understands Jesus to have been fully human and not omniscient.)[22] It is true that mass conversion of Gentiles to the new sect within Judaism took place only after the death of Jesus, but it is not true that this was all due to the activity of Paul. Jesus' intimate group of Galilean disciples, including Peter, John and Philip, was also involved. The disagreements that arose within the primitive church concerned what initiation and cultic rites should be required of the Gentiles who were converted, not the issue of Gentile conversion itself.

Dawkins's criticism of Jesus for promoting "dodgy family values" is perhaps more understandable.[23] Dawkins is right to identify a redefinition of family priorities as one of the radical demands that Jesus makes of his followers. Jesus in effect relocates and redefines the family in relation to himself, and—by the way—extends it to welcome out-groups. However, it must be emphasized that much of Jesus' teaching upheld family values and relationships, including the restoration of family relationships through his healing ministry.

A few examples will illustrate this point. Jesus' teaching about "Corban" (Mark 7:11) represents both a critique of a religious tradition that had lost its way and an affirmation of family responsibilities. The idea of "Corban" (an offering to the temple) appears to have been misused, allowing a son to claim justification in not supporting his parents in their old age simply because he had designated his property (or a part of it) as a gift to the temple. This strongly affirms the importance of caring for one's parents—a point reinforced by Jesus' concern to ensure his mother was cared for after his crucifixion (John 19:26-27). This concern for family life is also reflected in Jesus' insistence on the importance of marriage and the need to value children (Mark 10:1-16). Many readers would also point out that the parable of the prodigal son (Luke 15:11-32) presents a restored family relationship between a father and his son as a positive analogy for the themes of the gospel.

Interestingly, Dawkins believes that it is important that Western culture should not eliminate the Bible from educational programs. "We can give up belief in God while not losing touch with a treasured heritage."[24] Why, then, does he misrepresent one of the most central, influential and ethically significant parts of that "treasured heritage"—the teaching of Jesus of Nazareth? It does not require anything more than a basic familiarity with the gospels to realize that Dawkins's account of the teaching of Jesus of Nazareth is open to challenge. The cultural issue here is not whether what Jesus said is right; it is to be right about what Jesus said.

CHRISTIANITY AND THE CRITIQUE OF RELIGION

Dawkins's failure to distinguish between "belief in God" and "religion" makes it difficult for him to understand one of the most important themes of both the Hebrew Scriptures and the Gospels— the critique of religion. One of the great themes of the prophetic tradition of the Hebrew Scriptures (not touched upon, by the way, in Dawkins's excoriation of the Bible) is that Israel's religion has become corrupted and detached from faithful obedience to a God who loves justice, mercy, and personal integrity.[25] The nature of God constitutes a standpoint outside religion from which religious practices may be judged.

This theme can be found in the prophetic writings dating from eight centuries before Christ, and is intrinsic to the nature of Old Testament religion. The prophetic tradition is predominantly (though not exclusively) in tension with the cult throughout the Old Testament, especially where the priestly cult and the king are seen to have lost the spirit of the law, and the powerful are exploiting the weak. In an important critique of the cult, the prophet Micah compares the cultic demands for "burnt offerings" or "thousands of rams" with God's real requirement: to "do justice, and to love kindness, and to walk humbly with your God" (Micah 6:6-8). Or the prophet Isaiah's criticism was that Israel was so obsessed with cultic rituals that they had failed to "rescue the oppressed, defend the orphan, plead for the widow" (Isaiah 1:12-17).

Dawkins is right when he argues that it is necessary to critique religion; yet he appears unaware that it possesses internal means of reform and renewal. This is especially evident in the ministry of Jesus of Nazareth, where it often took the form of the criticism or flagrant transgression of cultic regulations or ritual practices, where these were coming between God and his people. The breaking of sabbath regulations exemplifies this well. The phenomenon of religion is a provisional, human institution, which is open to reform and renewal. Jesus' mission was to challenge the religious forms of his day, and, in the end, that is what led to him being crucified.

ON READING THE OLD TESTAMENT

From what has already been said, it will be clear that Dawkins takes a strongly negative attitude toward the Bible, based on a generally superficial engagement with its core themes and ideas, and an inadequate knowledge of the text itself. When Dawkins tells us that St. Paul wrote the letter to the Hebrews, you realize just how bad things are.[26]

His highly selective discussion of the Hebrew Scriptures in particular is peppered with outrage and indignation, which many of his readers will possibly share.[27] One can understand the bewilderment that Dawkins experiences in reading passages from the Torah that he holds to imply misogyny, vindictiveness to enemies and an incomprehensible emphasis on such odd obsessions as blood sacrifice and ritual purity.

Of course, many modern Jewish and non-Jewish readers find many parts of the Hebrew Scriptures puzzling, perhaps appalling, through their cultural distance from a long-past era. Historically, it

is important to appreciate that these ancient texts arose within a
people who were fighting to maintain their group or national identity in the face of onslaughts from all sides, who were making
sense of their human situation in relation to a God about whose
nature their thinking became more and more developed in the
millennium over which the material that makes up these Scriptures was being produced, orally and in writing. (Dawkins asserts
they were "chaotically cobbled together";[28] the evidence is that
they were carefully edited and reedited over many years.)

The passages that Dawkins finds so shocking appear alongside
other material in the Pentateuch, which he ignores, dealing with
forgiveness and compassion—the laws urging hospitality toward
strangers (Deuteronomy 10:17-19), setting limits on acts of revenge (Leviticus 19:18), prohibiting slavery (Leviticus 25:39-43),
declaring a jubilee for debt (Leviticus 25:25-28) and forbidding
infant sacrifice (Leviticus 18:21; 20:2). He also ignores the proph-
ets and the wisdom literature, in which the heights of Jewish
moral insight are expressed—insights that continue to shape and
nourish the human quest for moral values.

So how are we to make sense of the Hebrew Scriptures? Dawkins rightly demands that there should be an external criterion for
dealing with the interpretation of these texts.[29] Yet he seems unaware of the Christian insistence that there indeed exists such a
criterion—the life and teaching of Jesus of Nazareth.

Christians base this approach on the teaching of Jesus himself, who saw himself as having come to fulfill, not to abolish,
the Jewish law (Matthew 5:17). Dawkins takes the view that
Jesus regarded the Old Testament as wrong, requiring correc-

tion; Jesus, however, saw himself as fulfilling the Old Testament, thus transforming it. To use a familiar New Testament image, Jesus did not create the wine of the Gospels *de novo,* but took the water of the Jewish law and transmuted it to something better. The Hebrew Scriptures are read and interpreted through a Christological filter or prism. It is for this reason that Christians do not—and never have—implemented the cultic law set out in the pages of the Old Testament.[30]

True to form, Dawkins ignores this inconvenience, insisting that to take the Bible seriously is to "strictly observe the sabbath and think it just and proper to execute anyone who chose not to." Or to "execute disobedient children."[31] Dawkins knows this is not true; enough Christians have told him so. His repetition of this nonsense does him little credit and simply suggests that he expects his readers seriously to believe that Christians are in the habit of stoning people to death. A reality check is clearly in order.

RELIGION AND WELL-BEING

Until very recently, Dawkins persistently maintained that religion is bad for you. Over the last decade there has been an accumulation of observational evidence indicating—I think it is unwise to use a stronger word—that religious belief and commitment may have a generally positive influence on human well-being and longevity. It must be stressed, in the first place, that much more work remains to be done in this field, and, in the second, that this does not for one moment "prove" that religion is "right" (how could it?). Yet it does point to the growing importance of exploring the relation of spirituality to human well-being, unhindered by the ideological constraints of secular or religious polemics. And the evidence linking well-being to spirituality is growing. There are obvious implications here for public healthcare policy and practice. Why should spirituality be excluded from healthcare when it clearly matters so much to patients? On any goal-centered approach, it would clearly seem to be an appropriate inclusion. It's not what rampant secularists would like, but it's the way the evidence leads us.[32]

I challenged the accuracy of the slogan "religion is bad for you" in *Dawkins' God,* drawing attention to the growing body of evidence-based studies that showed it was nothing of the sort. Yet while now apparently conceding this point, Dawkins is unwilling to modify his antireligious polemics. His argument now seems to be something along the lines of "even if religion isn't *always* bad for you, that doesn't prove that it's true." Dawkins still persists in his representation of religion as characteristically, if not universally, malevolent. Yet, far from being based on objective scientific analysis, Dawkins's discussion of the impact of religion on mental health is based on anecdote, hearsay, creedal statements and discriminatory stereotyping.

Consider this representative statement: "It is hard to believe, for example, that health is improved by the semi-permanent state of morbid guilt suffered by a Roman Catholic possessed of normal human frailty and less than normal intelligence."[33] This is a Dawkins-eye view of things: I can't make sense of this—so it must be wrong. But truth is not determined by what Dawkins finds difficult to believe but by what the scientific, empirical evidence indicates—whether Dawkins likes this or not, or chooses to believe it or not. Just where in *The God Delusion* is the full discussion one has a right to expect of the significant body of scientific literature on the relationship of harmful and healthy aspects of religion—as seen, for example, in the extensive research work of Kenneth Pargament and his colleagues?[34] It's yet another example of Dawkins's pervasive cognitive bias, which accentuates the evidence he likes and overlooks or discounts that which he does not.

Dawkins is also highly critical of various religious practices that he regards as eccentric, pointless or harmful. He begins his list of examples of such objectionable religious practices with fasting.[35] Yet the intentional self-deprivation of food is a common feature of human life, whether it is undertaken from a religious or nonreligious perspective. In each case, one can identify "healthy" and "unhealthy" approaches, as table 4.1 illustrates.

Table 4.1. Healthy and Unhealthy Approaches to Fasting

	Religious	Nonreligious
Healthy	Fasting according to recognized practice of group. Achieving religious experience or insight that is recognized as being beneficial.	Cutting down on sugar, saturated fats and processed foods, caffeine, and alcohol. Achieving improved fitness, reduced blood pressure, feeling well.
Unhealthy	Radical reduction in caloric intake, along with feelings of self-loathing focused on body image supported by beliefs in or experiences of divine mandate. Achieving extreme weight loss, amenorrhea, heart failure, depression.	Radical reduction in caloric intake, along with feelings of self-loathing focused on body image. Achieving extreme weight loss, amenorrhea, heart failure, depression.

This shows that it is possible to consider the real difference between "religious" and "nonreligious" as lying not in the behavior
itself but in the meaning attributed to it and the goal to which it is
directed.[36] Furthermore, religious behavior is neither intrinsically
healthy nor intrinsically unhealthy.

Dawkins may argue that it seems to him that fasting serves no
useful purpose; yet this judgment arises out of a fundamental dis-
inclination on his part to allow that religion can be valid, helpful
or important, or that the achievement or enhancement of spiritual
goals can be personally satisfying and conducive to well-being.

Let me conclude this section with a wise comment from Michael
Shermer, president of the Skeptics Society. In exploring the contemporary resurgence of religion, Shermer noted that religions
were implicated in some human tragedies, such as holy wars.
While rightly castigating these—a criticism which I gladly echo—
Shermer goes on to make a point that most atheists I know would
endorse. There is clearly a significant positive side to religion:

> However, for every one of these grand tragedies there are ten
> thousand acts of personal kindness and social good that go
> unreported. . . . Religion, like all social institutions of such
> historical depth and cultural impact, cannot be reduced to
> an unambiguous good or evil.[37]

Why do so many thinking atheists endorse Shermer's comment?
Because that's exactly what the evidence shows.

Yet the pejorative and hostile spin relentlessly placed on religion
by Dawkins asserts that it is a universal, unambiguous evil that is a
dangerous threat to civilization. While Dawkins clearly regards

Shermer as a competent and sympathetic authority, to judge from his appeal to him in *The God Delusion,* he is unwilling to adopt the balanced and judicious analysis that Sherman presents.[38] Why not? I fear the answer is simple: because it doesn't make for the slick and simple soundbites that will reassure the godless faithful.

It is this feature of the work that has led to its mauling by so many informed critics on all sides of the debate. As Terry Eagleton comments, with a sarcasm reflecting his obvious exasperation at *The God Delusion's* risible caricatures of religion:

> Such is Dawkins's unruffled scientific impartiality that in a book of almost four hundred pages, he can scarcely bring himself to concede that a single human benefit has flowed from religious faith, a view which is as *a priori* improbable as it is empirically false.[39]

Atheism must indeed be in a sorry state if its leading contemporary defender has to depend so heavily—and so *obviously*—on the improbable and the false to bolster his case.

CONCLUSION

Every worldview, whether religious or not, has its point of vulnerability. There is a tension between theory and experience, raising questions over the coherence and trustworthiness of the worldview itself. In the case of Christianity, many locate that point of weakness in the existence of suffering within the world. In the case of atheism, it is the persistence of belief in God, when there is supposedly no God in which to believe.

Until recently, Western atheism had waited patiently, believing that belief in God would simply die out. But now, a whiff of panic is evident. Far from dying out, belief in God has rebounded and seems set to exercise still greater influence in both the public and private spheres. *The God Delusion* expresses this deep anxiety, partly reflecting an intense distaste for religion. Yet there is something deeper here, often overlooked in the heat of debate. The anxiety is that the coherence of atheism itself is at stake. Might the unexpected resurgence of religion persuade many that atheism itself is fatally flawed as a worldview?

The God Delusion seems more designed to reassure atheists whose faith is faltering than to engage fairly or rigorously with religious believers and others seeking for truth. (One wonders if this is because the writer is himself an atheist whose faith is faltering.) Religious believers will be dismayed by its ritual stereotyping of religion and will find its manifest lack of fairness a significant disincentive to take its arguments and concerns seriously. Seekers after truth who would not consider themselves religious may also find themselves shocked by Dawkins's aggressive rhetoric, his substitution of personal creedal statements for objective engagement with evidence, his hectoring and bullying tone toward "dyed-in-the-wool faith-heads" and his utter determination to find nothing but fault with religion of any kind.

It is this deep, unsettling anxiety about the future of atheism that explains the "high degree of dogmatism" and "aggressive rhetorical style" of this new secular fundamentalism.[40] Fundamentalism arises when a worldview feels it is in danger, lashing out at its enemies when it fears its own future is threatened. *The God Delusion* is a work of theater rather than scholarship—a fierce, rhetor-

ical assault on religion and passionate plea for it to be banished to
the lunatic fringes of society, where it can do no harm. None can
doubt the visceral appeal that this book will make to a secular audience that is alarmed at the new political importance attached to
religion and its growing influence and presence in the public
arena. Its dismissive attitude to religion will doubtless win plau-
dits from those who heartily dislike religion.

Yet others have been more cautious. Aware of the moral obliga-
tion of a critic of religion to deal with this phenomenon at its best
and most persuasive, many have been disturbed by Dawkins's
crude stereotypes, vastly oversimplified binary oppositions (science is good; religion is bad), straw men and hostility toward religion. Might *The God Delusion* actually backfire and end up per-
suading people that atheism is just as intolerant, doctrinaire and
disagreeable as the worst that religion can offer?

Dawkins seems to think that saying something more loudly and
confidently, while ignoring or trivializing counterevidence, will persuade the open-minded that religious belief is a type of delusion.
Sadly, sociological studies of charismatic leaders—religious and secular—indicate that Dawkins may be right to place some hope in this
strategy. For the gullible and credulous, it is the confidence with
which something is said that persuades rather than the evidence offered in its support. Yet the fact that Dawkins relies so excessively
on rhetoric rather than the evidence that would otherwise be his
natural stock in trade clearly indicates that something is wrong with
his case. Ironically the ultimate achievement of *The God Delusion* for
modern atheism may be to suggest that this emperor has no clothes
to wear. Might *atheism* be a delusion about God?

Notes

INTRODUCTION

[1]Richard Dawkins, *The God Delusion* (Boston: Houghton Mifflin, 2006).

[2]Ibid., p. 5.

[3]Michael Shermer, *How We Believe: Science, Skepticism, and the Search for God* (New York: Freeman, 2000), pp. 16-31.

[4]Stephen Jay Gould, "Impeaching a Self-Appointed Judge." *Scientific American* 267, no. 1 (1992): 118-21.

[5]For some such books see C. S. Lewis, *Mere Christianity* (New York: Macmillan, 1984); and N. T. Wright, *Simply Christian* (San Francisco: HarperSanFrancisco, 2006).

[6]Readers who would appreciate a more extended scholarly and analytical engagement with Dawkins's "scientific atheism" should read Alister E. McGrath, *Dawkins' God: Genes, Memes and the Meaning of Life* (Malden, Mass.: Blackwell, 2004). While this book represents a sympathetic yet critical study of Dawkins's views on science and religion up to 2004, *The God Delusion* develops a broader range of arguments, which clearly invite further evaluation and response.

CHAPTER 1: DELUDED ABOUT GOD?

[1]Richard Dawkins, *The God Delusion* (Boston: Houghton Mifflin, 2006), p. 38.

[2]This definition dates back to 1976, when it appeared in *The Selfish Gene.* See Richard Dawkins, *The Selfish Gene,* 2nd ed. (Oxford: Oxford University Press, 1989), p. 198.

[3]Dawkins, *God Delusion,* p. 308.

[4]A much more sophisticated account of the origins of belief, bearing some slight resemblance to that offered by Dawkins, is found in the writings of Sigmund Freud. Dawkins shows no awareness of this and makes no reference to Freud in *The God Delusion.*

[5]Dawkins, *God Delusion,* pp. 325-37.

[6]Terry Eagleton, "Lunging, Flailing, Mispunching: A Review of Richard Dawkins' *The God Delusion,*" *London Review of Books,* October 19, 2006.

[7]Nicholas Humphrey, cited in Dawkins, *God Delusion,* p. 326.

[8]Dawkins, *God Delusion,* p. 5.

[9]Richard Dawkins, *A Devil's Chaplain: Reflections on Hope, Lies, Science, and Love* (Boston: Houghton Mifflin, 2003), p. 139.

[10]Dawkins, *God Delusion,* p. 190. The Web source provided is a list of citations, all in English translation, without the original German or Latin, any indication of their sources and making no attempt at scholarly engagement.

[11]For a more careful account see Alister E. McGrath, *Luther's Theology of the Cross: Martin Luther's Theological Breakthrough* (Oxford: Blackwell, 1985).

[12]Richard Dawkins, *The Blind Watchmaker: Why the Evidence of Evolution Reveals a Universe Without Design* (New York: W. W. Norton, 1986).

[13]See the points made by David O'Connor, "On Failing to Resolve Theism-Versus-Atheism Empirically," *Religious Studies* 26 (1990): 91-103.

[14]Dawkins, *God Delusion,* pp. 77-79.

[15]For the importance of this point, see Samuel P. Huntington and Lawrence E. Harrison, eds., *Culture Matters: How Values Shape Human Progress* (New York: Basic, 2000).

[16]Dawkins himself makes this point: "We must acknowledge the possibility that new facts may come to light which will force our successors of the twenty-first century to abandon Darwinism or modify it beyond recognition" (*A Devil's Chaplain* [London: Weidenfeld & Nicolson, 2003], p. 81).

[17]Dawkins, *God Delusion,* pp. 111-59.

[18]Ibid., p. 109.

[19]Ibid., p. 77.

[20]Among the best introductions, see David Deutsch, *The Fabric of Reality* (New York: Allen Lane, 1997); and Brian Greene, *The Elegant Universe: Superstrings, Hidden Dimensions, and the Quest for the Ultimate Theory* (New York: Norton, 2000).

[21]Richard Dawkins, *Climbing Mount Improbable* (New York: Norton, 1996).

[22]Dawkins, *God Delusion,* pp. 125-34. Dawkins here focuses on the intelligent design movement.

[23]See the account in David J. Hawkin and Eileen Hawkin, *The Word of Science: The Religious and Social Thought of C. A. Coulson* (London: Epworth, 1989).

[24]Dawkins, *God Delusion,* p. 126.

[25]Dawkins, *Devil's Chaplain,* p. 19.

[26]Richard Swinburne, *Is There a God?* (Oxford: Oxford University Press, 1996).

CHAPTER 2: HAS SCIENCE DISPROVED GOD?

[1]Stephen Jay Gould, "Impeaching a Self-Appointed Judge," *Scientific American* 267, no. 1 (1992). For a more extended discussion of the issues, see Stephen Jay Gould, *Rocks of Ages: Science and Religion in the Fullness of Life* (New York: Ballantine, 2002).

[2]Richard Dawkins, *The God Delusion* (Boston: Houghton Mifflin, 2006), p. 57.

[3]For Dawkins's response, which hardly addresses the issue, see ibid., p. 56.

[4]I take this from one of the best recent studies of this question: Peter Lipton, *Inference to the Best Explanation,* 2nd ed. (New York: Routledge, 2004), p. 5.

[5]For a particularly bold statement of this approach, see Peter Atkins, "The Limitless Power of Science," in *Nature's Imagination: The Frontiers of Scientific Vision,* ed. John Cornwell (Oxford: Oxford University Press, 1995), pp. 122-32.

[6]Richard Dawkins, *The Selfish Gene* (Oxford: Oxford University Press, 1976), p. 21.

[7]Denis Noble, *The Music of Life: Biology Beyond the Genome* (Oxford: Oxford University Press, 2006), pp. 11-15.

[8]Ibid., p. 13; see also Richard Dawkins, *The Extended Phenotype: The Gene as the Unit of Selection* (New York: Oxford University Press, 1982), p. 1.

[9]M. R. Bennett and P. M. S. Hacker, *Philosophical Foundations of Neuroscience*

(Malden, Mass.: Blackwell, 2003), pp. 372-76.

[10]Ibid., p. 374: "It is wrong-headed to suppose that the only forms of explanation are scientific." The entire section dealing with reductionism (pp. 355-77) merits close study.

[11]Peter B. Medawar, *The Limits of Science* (Oxford: Oxford University Press, 1985), p. 66.

[12]See, for example, the illuminating discussion in Luke Davidson, "Fragilities of Scientism: Richard Dawkins and the Paranoid Idealization of Science," *Science as Culture* 9 (2000): 167-99. The best discussion to date of this phenomenon is Mikael Stenmark, *Scientism: Science, Ethics and Religion* (Williston, Vt.: Ashgate, 2001). Dawkins and E. O. Wilson are here treated as the leading representatives of the movement. Dawkins considers himself not to be "narrowly scientistic" (Dawkins, *God Delusion,* p. 155).

[13]Dawkins, *God Delusion,* p. 56.

[14]Francis S. Collins, *The Language of God* (New York: Free Press, 2006), p. 6.

[15]For an introduction, see Alister E. McGrath, *The Science of God* (Grand Rapids: Eerdmans, 2004).

[16]See especially Roy Bhaskar, *The Possibility of Naturalism: A Philosophical Critique of the Contemporary Human Sciences,* 3rd ed. (New York: Routledge, 1998).

[17]Owen Gingerich, *God's Universe* (Cambridge, Mass.: Harvard University Press, 2006).

[18]Dawkins, *God Delusion,* p. 152.

[19]Ibid.

[20]See the disappointingly superficial analysis in *God Delusion,* pp. 14-18. Dawkins speaks of "Einsteinian pantheism" (which is certainly one aspect of Einstein's religious ideas), while failing to realize that pantheism is both a religious and theological notion. For a good analysis, see Michael P. Levine, *Pantheism: A Non-Theistic Concept of Deity* (New York: Routledge, 1994).

[21]Dawkins, *God Delusion,* pp. 279-86.

[22]Ibid., pp. 66-69.

[23]Ruse's best work, in my view, is *Monad to Man: The Concept of Progress in Evolutionary Biology* (Cambridge, Mass.: Harvard University Press, 1996).

[24]Dawkins, *God Delusion,* p. 67.

[25]Dawkins insists that he is not an atheist fundamentalist (see *God Delusion,* p.

282). This is very contestable!

[26]Ibid., pp. 131-34, with reference to Michael Behe; William Dembski is not mentioned. For a somewhat more informed engagement with the movement, see Niall Shanks, *God, the Devil, and Darwin: A Critique of Intelligent Design Theory* (New York: Oxford University Press, 2004).

[27]For Dembski's approach, see William A. Dembski, *Intelligent Design: The Bridge Between Science & Theology* (Downers Grove, Ill.: InterVarsity Press, 1999).

[28]See Madeleine Bunting's perceptive article "Why the Intelligent Design Lobby Thanks God for Richard Dawkins," *The Guardian* [London], March 27, 2006.

[29]For Ruse's Darwinism, see Michael Ruse, *Taking Darwin Seriously: A Naturalistic Approach to Philosophy* (New York: Prometheus, 1998). The exchange of e-mails between Ruse and Dennett took place on February 19, 2006, and was widely distributed.

[30]For Ruse's assessment of this statement, see Michael Ruse, "John Paul II and Evolution," *Quarterly Review of Biology* 72 (1997): 391-95.

[31]Michael Ruse, cited in Dawkins, *God Delusion*, p. 67.

CHAPTER 3: WHAT ARE THE ORIGINS OF RELIGION?

[1]Richard Dawkins, *The God Delusion* (Boston: Houghton Mifflin, 2006), pp. 51-54. The idea is borrowed from Bertrand Russell.

[2]See Van A. Harvey, *Feuerbach and the Interpretation of Religion* (Cambridge: Cambridge University Press, 1995).

[3]Sigmund Freud, *Totem and Taboo: Resemblances Between the Psychic Lives of Savages and Neurotics* (New York: Moffat Yard, 1918).

[4]Daniel C. Dennett, *Breaking the Spell: Religion as a Natural Phenomenon* (New York: Viking Penguin, 2006).

[5]See the original study of Charles Y. Glock and Rodney Stark, *Religion and Society in Tension* (Chicago: Rand McNally, 1965). The anthropologist Talal Asad argues that "there cannot be a universal definition of religion, not only because its constituent elements and relationships are historically specific, but because that definition is itself the historical product of discursive processes" (Talal Asad, *Genealogies of Religion* [Baltimore: Johns Hopkins University Press 1993], p. 29).

[6]Dawkins, *God Delusion*, p. 188.

[7]Richard Dawkins, *River Out of Eden: A Darwinian View of Life* (New York: Basic, 1995), p. 133.

[8]Dawkins, *God Delusion,* pp. 31-38.

[9]See, for example, Ernest Gellner, *Muslim Society* (Cambridge: Cambridge University Press, 1981), pp. 9-11, which extends David Hume's notion of the "flux and reflux" of polytheism and monotheism to suggest that a natural part of human experience is a cyclical movement from polytheism to monotheism—and then back again.

[10]Dawkins, *God Delusion,* pp. 161-207. In terms of the substance of Dawkins's intellectual case against religion, this is the most important chapter in the book.

[11]See, for example, Peter Harrison, *"Religion" and the Religions in the English Enlightenment* (Cambridge: Cambridge University Press, 1990); Tomoko Masuzawa, *In Search of Dreamtime: The Quest for the Origin of Religion* (Chicago: University of Chicago Press, 1993); Daniel L. Pals, *Seven Theories of Religion* (New York: Oxford University Press, 1996); and Samuel J. Preus, *Explaining Religion: Criticism and Theory from Bodin to Freud* (New Haven, Conn.: Yale University Press, 1987).

[12]Peter B. Clarke and Peter Byrne, *Religion Defined and Explained* (New York: St. Martin's Press, 1993), pp. 3-27.

[13]Dawkins, *God Delusion,* p. 188.

[14]See Eric Csapo, *Theories of Mythology* (Malden, Mass.: Blackwell, 2005), pp. 36-43.

[15]Dawkins, *God Delusion,* p. 166.

[16]For a recent study of cognitive bias in relation to self-esteem, see Jennifer Crocker and Lora E. Park, "The Costly Pursuit of Self-Esteem," *Psychological Bulletin* 130 (2004): 392-414.

[17]A classic study of this theme is Robert P. Carroll, *When Prophecy Failed: Cognitive Dissonance in the Prophetic Traditions of the Old Testament* (New York: Seabury, 1979).

[18]See for instance Rodney Stark and Charles Y. Glock, *American Piety: The Nature of Religious Commitment* (Berkeley: University of California Press, 1968).

[19]John D. Teasdale and Philip J. Barnard, *Affect, Cognition, and Change: Re-modelling Depressive Thought* (Mahwah, N.J.: Erlbaum, 1993).

[20]See the analysis in Alister E. McGrath, *The Genesis of Doctrine* (Oxford: Blackwell, 1990).

[21]For some interesting experimental work in this area see N. J. Gibson, *The Experimental Investigation of Religious Cognition* (Ph.D. diss., University of Cambridge, 2006).

[22]Dawkins, *God Delusion,* pp. 168-69.

[23]Ibid., p. 179.

[24]Bennett and Hacker, *Philosophical Foundations of Neuroscience,* pp. 127, 243. For a detailed study of the "mereological fallacy," see ibid., pp. 68-107. (Mereology is the logic of the relationship between the whole and its constituent parts.)

[25]Dawkins, *God Delusion,* pp. 182-84. For a critique of the ideas set out here, see Bennett and Hacker, *Philosophical Foundations of Neuroscience,* pp. 419-27.

[26]Jeffrey L. Saver and John Rabin, "The Neural Substrates of Religious Experience," *Journal of Neuropsychiatry & Clinical Neurosciences* 9 (1997): 498-510.

[27]Michael A. Persinger, *Neuropsychological Bases of God Beliefs* (New York: Praeger, 1987). Dawkins does not appear to be familiar with this work at first hand, providing indirect reference (*God Delusion,* p. 168) through Michael Shermer's *How We Believe* (New York: Henry Holt, 2000). He offers no critical assessment of the validity of the hypothesis.

[28]Peter Fenwick, "The Neurophysiology of Religious Experiences," in *Psychiatry and Religion: Context, Consensus, and Controversies,* ed. D. Bhugra (London: Routledge, 1996), pp. 167-77.

[29]Fraser Watts, "Cognitive Neuroscience and Religious Consciousness," in *Neuroscience and the Person,* ed. R. J. Murphy et al. (Vatican City: Vatican Observatory, 1999), pp. 327-46.

[30]"Could irrational religion be a by-product of the irrationality mechanisms that were originally built into the brain by selection for falling in love?" (Dawkins, *God Delusion,* p. 185). It is an interesting suggestion, though one that is simply not sustained by the very limited evidence Dawkins bothers to present, which is in any case inattentive to the extent to which "falling in love" is a culturally conditioned notion.

[31]Antoine Vergote, "What the Psychology of Religion Is and What It Is Not," *International Journal for the Psychology of Religion* 3 (1993): 73-86.

[32]For my comments, see McGrath, *Dawkins' God* (Malden, Mass.: Blackwell, 2004), pp. 135-38.

[33]Dawkins, *God Delusion,* pp. 186, 188.

[34]Ibid., pp. 191-201.

[35]Richard Dawkins, *The Selfish Gene,* 2nd ed (Oxford: Oxford University Press, 1989), p. 193.

[36]For an extended analysis of Dawkins's concept of the meme, see McGrath, *Dawkins' God,* pp. 119-35.

[37]This point was made forcefully by James W. Polichak, "Memes—What Are They Good For?" *Skeptic* 6, no. 3 (1998): 45-54. Polichak's concerns were not met by Susan J. Blackmore, *The Meme Machine* (New York: Oxford University Press, 1999). See further Bennett and Hacker, *Philosophical Foundations of Neuroscience,* pp. 431-35.

[38]Maurice Bloch, "A Well-Disposed Social Anthropologist's Problem with Memes," in *Darwinizing Culture: The Status of Memetics as a Science,* ed. Robert Aunger (Oxford: Oxford University Press, 2000), pp. 189-203.

[39]For examples of such models, see Michael Carrithers, *Why Humans Have Cultures: Explaining Anthropology and Social Diversity* (Oxford: Oxford University Press, 1996); and Maurice Bloch, *How We Think They Think: Anthropological Approaches to Cognition, Memory, and Literacy* (Boulder, Colo.: Westview, 1998). Even biologists have problems with the idea. As Simon Conway Morris, professor of evolutionary palaeobiology at Cambridge University, pointed out, memes seem to have no place in serious scientific reflection. "Memes are trivial, to be banished by simple mental exercises. In any wider context, they are hopelessly, if not hilariously, simplistic" (Simon Conway Morris, *Life's Solution: Inevitable Humans in a Lonely Universe* [Cambridge: Cambridge University Press, 2003], p. 324).

[40]Dawkins, *God Delusion,* p. 196.

[41]Ibid., p. 250. His own view seems to be that Jesus probably did exist (ibid., p. 97). The reasons for this important judgment are not stated or defended.

[42]See Alan Costall, "The 'Meme' Meme," *Cultural Dynamics* 4 (1991): 321-35.

CHAPTER 4: IS RELIGION EVIL?

[1]Richard Dawkins, *The God Delusion* (Boston: Houghton Mifflin, 2006), p. 31.

[2]See ibid., pp. 301-7.

[3]Ibid., pp. 329-31.

[4]For a good discussion, see Keith Ward, *Is Religion Dangerous?* (Oxford: Lion, 2006).

[5]Anna Dickinson, "Quantifying Religious Oppression: Russian Orthodox Church Closures and Repression of Priests 1917-41," *Religion, State & Society* 28 (2000): 327-35.

[6]Dawkins, *God Delusion,* p. 249 (italics added).

[7]Alexandru D. Popescu, *Petre Tutea: Between Sacrifice and Suicide* (Williston, Vt.: Ashgate, 2004).

[8]Dawkins, *God Delusion,* pp. 303-4.

[9]Others include Daniel C. Dennett, *Breaking the Spell* (New York: Viking Penguin, 2006); and Sam Harris, *The End of Faith: Religion, Terror, and the Future of Reason* (New York: Free Press, 2006).

[10]Robert A. Pape, *Dying to Win: The Strategic Logic of Suicide Terrorism* (New York: Random House, 2005). See also the nuanced discussions in Diego Gambetta, ed., *Making Sense of Suicide Missions* (Oxford: Oxford University Press, 2005).

[11]See the important study of Malise Ruthven, *Fundamentalism: The Search for Meaning* (Oxford: Oxford University Press, 2004).

[12]For an illustration of the importance of the device, see Kathy Mills, "Deconstructing Binary Oppositions in Literacy Discourse and Pedagogy," *Australian Journal of Language and Literacy* 28 (2005): 67-82.

[13]See Michael Wheeler, *The Old Enemies: Catholic and Protestant in Nineteenth-Century English Culture* (Cambridge: Cambridge University Press, 2006).

[14]See the analysis in Stephen E. Cornell and Douglas Hartmann, *Ethnicity and Race: Making Identities in a Changing World* (Thousand Oaks, Calif.: Pine Forge, 1998); Fredrik Barth, *Ethnic Groups and Boundaries: The Social Organization of Culture Difference* (Prospect Heights, Ill.: Waveland, 1998); and Jane Hubert, *Madness, Disability, and Social Exclusion: The Archaeology and Anthropology of "Difference"* (New York: Routledge, 2000).

[15]Dawkins, *God Delusion,* p. 259.

[16]See the brilliant study of Edward Muir, *Mad Blood Stirring: Vendetta in Renaissance Italy* (Baltimore: Johns Hopkins University Press, 1998).

[17]Bruce E. Blaine, *The Psychology of Diversity: Perceiving and Experiencing Social Difference* (Mountain View, Calif.: Mayfield , 2000).

[18]This theme is particularly emphasized by Émile Durkheim, *The Elementary Forms of the Religious Life* (New York: Macmillan, 1926).

[19]Dawkins, *God Delusion,* p. 257.

[20]Dawkins cites the Jewish prayer thanking God for not making the supplicant a Gentile, a woman or a slave (ibid., p. 259). He fails to point out that Jesus repudiated such sentiments (Luke 18:9-14).

[21]See Jeremy Duff and Joanna Collicutt McGrath, *Meeting Jesus: Human Responses to a Yearning God* (London: SPCK, 2006), pp. 20-25, 58-62.

[22]Theologically alert readers will note that Dawkins seems docetic in his understanding of Christ at this point (*God Delusion,* p. 253).

[23]Dawkins, *God Delusion,* pp. 250-51.

[24]Ibid., p. 344.

[25]The issue is dealt with in all standard histories of Israelite religion. See, for example, Patrick D. Miller, *The Religion of Ancient Israel* (Louisville, Ky.: Westminster John Knox, 2000).

[26]Dawkins, *God Delusion,* p. 253. It has been accepted for several centuries that the author of this letter is not Paul. Other errors and misunderstandings include the bald statement that original sin "lies at the heart of New Testament theology" (p. 251). It does not; it is an Augustinian development, dating from centuries later. Jesus rarely talked about sin at all, and he certainly did not link it with Adam. Jesus' notion of forgiveness was really about liberation from bondage, not moral exoneration. On the face of it, Paul talks quite a lot about sin in the first half of his letter to the Romans. Yet his point is not so much that all have *sinned* but that *all* have sinned. His agenda is to establish a level playing field between Jew and Gentile. Dawkins also fails to understand the genre of apocalyptic, as found in the book of Revelation, which Dawkins dismisses as one of the "weirdest books in the Bible." He represents the interpretations of this book associated with the Jehovah's Witnesses as normative for Christianity—for example, the assertion that none of the saved could be women. The 144,000 "sealed" are not identical with the "saved" (p. 257), in that people from every tribe and tongue are saved (Revelation 7:9; 14:6). The 144,000 are probably Christian ascetic "warriors" who are using pacifist means and spiritual warfare to resist secular atheist powers and cosmic evil powers.

[27]Twelve of the fourteen references Dawkins cites are taken from the Pentateuch or Torah. The remaining two are from Judges; none are cited from the remaining thirty-six books of the Old Testament.

[28]Dawkins, *God Delusion,* p. 237.

[29]Ibid., p. 243.

[30]For its basic elements, see Joel Marcus, *The Way of the Lord: Christological Exegesis of the Old Testament in the Gospel of Mark* (Louisville, Ky.: Westminster John Knox, 1992).

[31]Dawkins, *God Delusion*, pp. 249-50.

[32]See, for example, David Myers, "The Funds, Friends and Faith of Happy People," *American Psychologist* 55 (2000): 56-67; Harold G. Koenig and Harvey J. Cohen, *The Link Between Religion and Health: Psychoneuroimmunology and the Faith Factor* (New York: Oxford University Press, 2002); Marc Galanter, *Spirituality and the Healthy Mind: Science, Therapy, and the Need for Personal Meaning* (New York: Oxford University Press, 2005).

[33]Dawkins, *God Delusion*, p. 167.

[34]Kenneth I. Pargament, *The Psychology of Religion and Coping: Theory, Research, Practice* (New York: Guilford Press, 1997); Kenneth I. Pargament et al., "Patterns of Positive and Negative Religious Coping with Major Life Stressors," *Journal for the Scientific Study of Religion* 37 (1998): 710-24.

[35]Dawkins, *God Delusion*, p. 166.

[36]See especially Nicholas Lash, *Easter In Ordinary: Reflections on Human Experience and the Knowledge of God* (Charlottesville: University Press of Virginia, 1988).

[37]Michael Shermer, *How We Believe* (New York: Freeman, 2000), p. 71.

[38]Dawkins, *God Delusion*, p. 102 (see also pp. 127, 168), citing approvingly Shermer's *How We Believe*.

[39]Terry Eagleton, "Lunging, Flailing, Mispunching: A Review of Richard Dawkins' *The God Delusion*," *London Review of Books*, October 19, 2006. For Eagleton's own perceptive and critical comments on this important issue, see Terry Eagleton, *Holy Terror* (New York: Oxford University Press, 2005).

[40]See the points made by Nicholas D. Kristof, "A Modest Proposal for a Truce on Religion," *New York Times*, December 3, 2006.

For Further Reading

WHAT FOLLOWS ARE SOME BASIC WORKS that readers will find helpful in taking the issues raised in this book further. This list is not intended to be exhaustive. It is simply an indication of some useful starting points.

INTRODUCING RICHARD DAWKINS

Grafen, Alan, and Mark Ridley, eds. *Richard Dawkins: How a Scientist Changed the Way We Think: Reflections by Scientists, Writers, and Philosophers*. New York: Oxford University Press, 2006. A slightly uneven collection of essays about Dawkins.

McGrath, Alister E. *Dawkins' God: Genes, Memes and the Meaning of Life*. Malden, Mass.: Blackwell, 2004. The only book-length

study to date to examine the scientific, historical, philosophical
and theological aspects of Dawkins's attitude to religion.

Ridley, Mark. *Evolution.* 3rd ed. Malden, Mass.: Blackwell Science,
2003. Probably the best introduction to contemporary evolutionary theory currently available.

Shanahan, Timothy. "Methodological and Contextual Factors in
the Dawkins/Gould Dispute over Evolutionary Progress." *Studies in History and Philosophy of Science* 31 (2001): 127-51. A sophisticated analysis of Dawkins and Gould.

Sterelny, Kim. *Dawkins vs. Gould: Survival of the Fittest.* Cambridge:
Icon, 2001. An interesting and accessible comparison of Daw-
kins and Stephen Jay Gould on how best to understand the
Darwinian approach to evolution.

CHRISTIAN BELIEF

McGrath, Alister E. *Christian Theology: An Introduction.* 4th ed.
Malden, Mass.: Blackwell, 2007. The most widely used text-
book of Christian theology, which sets out what Christians believe and why clearly and impartially.

RELIGION AND WELL-BEING

Galanter, Marc. *Spirituality and the Healthy Mind: Science, Therapy,
and the Need for Personal Meaning.* New York: Oxford University
Press, 2005.

Koenig, Harold G., and Harvey J. Cohen. *The Link Between Religion
and Health: Psychoneuroimmunology and the Faith Factor.* New
York: Oxford University Press, 2002.

Miller, W. R., and C. E. Thoreson. "Spirituality, Religion and

Health: An Emerging Research Field." *American Psychologist* 58 (2003): 24-35.

Pargament, Kenneth I. *The Psychology of Religion and Coping: Theory, Research, Practice*. New York: Guilford, 1997.

Weaver, A. J., et al. "A Systematic Review of Research on Religion and Spirituality in *The Journal of Traumatic Stress*, 1990-99." *Mental Health, Religion and Culture* 6 (2003): 215-28.

RELIGION AND VIOLENCE

Eagleton, Terry. *Holy Terror*. New York: Oxford University Press, 2005.

Gambetta, Diego, ed. *Making Sense of Suicide Missions*. Oxford: Oxford University Press, 2005.

Kakar, Sudhir. *The Colors of Violence: Cultural Identities, Religion, and Conflict*. Chicago: University of Chicago Press, 1996.

Martin, David. *Does Christianity Cause War?* Oxford: Clarendon, 1997.

Pape, Robert A. *Dying to Win: The Strategic Logic of Suicide Terrorism*. New York: Random House, 2005.

Rosenbaum, Ron. *Explaining Hitler: The Search for the Origins of His Evil*. New York: Random House, 1998.

Stark, Rodney. *For the Glory of God: How Monotheism Led to Reformations, Science, Witch-hunts, and the End of Slavery*. Princeton, N.J.: Princeton University Press, 2003.

Ward, Keith. *Is Religion Dangerous?* Oxford: Lion, 2006.

THE PSYCHOLOGY OF RELIGION

Spilka, Bernard, et al. *The Psychology of Religion: An Empirical Ap-*

proach. 3rd ed. New York: Guilford, 2003.

Watts, Fraser, and Mark Williams. *The Psychology of Religious Knowing*. Cambridge: Cambridge University Press, 1988.

Wulff, David M. *Psychology of Religion: Classic and Contemporary*. 2nd ed. New York: Wiley, 1997.

THE RELATION OF SCIENCE AND RELIGION

It is important to read some reliable and up-to-date accounts of the contemporary understanding of the relation of science to religion in assessing Dawkins's biased and skewed misrepresentations. The best such studies include:

Alexander, Denis. *Rebuilding the Matrix: Science and Faith in the 21st Century*. Grand Rapids: Zondervan, 2002.

Barbour, Ian G. *When Science Meets Religion*. San Francisco: HarperSanFrancisco, 2000.

Brooke, John Hedley. *Science and Religion: Some Historical Perspectives*. Cambridge: Cambridge University Press, 1991.

———. *Telling the Story of Science and Religion: A Nuanced Account*. Cambridge: Cambridge University Press, 1991.

Collins, Francis S. *The Language of God: A Scientist Presents Evidence for Belief*. New York: Basic, 2006.

Gingerich, Owen. *God's Universe*. Cambridge, Mass.: Harvard University Press, 2006.

Lindberg, David C., and Ronald L. Numbers. *God and Nature: Historical Essays on the Encounter Between Christianity and Science*. Berkeley: University of California Press, 1986.

Nasr, Seyyed Hossein. *Religion and the Order of Nature*. Oxford: Oxford University Press, 1996.

Polkinghorne, John C. *Faith, Science and Understanding*. New Haven, Conn.: Yale University Press, 2000.

Ruse, Michael. *Can a Darwinian Be a Christian? The Relationship Between Science and Religion*. Cambridge: Cambridge University Press, 2001.

Ward, Keith. *Pascal's Fire: Scientific Faith and Religious Understanding*. Oxford: Oneworld, 2006.

About the Authors

THE DAWKINS DELUSION? **HAS MOSTLY BEEN WRITTEN** by Alister McGrath, presently professor of historical theology at Oxford University, and senior research fellow of Harris Manchester College. His primary interest is the history of Christian thought, with a particular emphasis on the relation between the natural sciences and Christian belief. He used to be an atheist, and attributes his lapse partly to the discovery of the philosophy of science and partly to a belated decision to investigate what Christianity really was, rather than accepting the stereotypes offered by his atheist friends (not a few of which recur in *The God Delusion*). After studying chemistry at Oxford, he researched in the field of molecular biophysics, developing new methods for investigating biological membranes. He then moved on to study Christian theology, specializing in the history of Christian thought and especially in issues of science and religion. A prolific author, his recent publications include *Dawkins' God: Genes, Memes and the Meaning of Life* (Blackwell, 2004).

Joanna Collicutt McGrath studied experimental psychology at Oxford, then went on to specialize for some years in clinical neuropsychology and subsequently studied Christian theology, specializing in biblical studies. Currently lecturer in the psychology of religion at Heythrop College, University of London, she has been involved in the whole of this work, but has made a particular contribution to those sections dealing with biblical studies and the relationship of religion with psychology and the neurosciences. Her book *Meeting Jesus: Human Responses to a Yearning God*, co-written with Jeremy Duff, was published by SPCK in 2006.